Myst™

Official Strategy Guide

NOW AVAILABLE

VIDEO GAME BOOKS

Nintendo Games Secrets, Volumes 1,
2, 3, and 4
Super NES Games Secrets, Volumes 1, 2, 3, and 4
Super Mario World Game Secrets
Nintendo Game Boy Secrets, Volumes 1 and 2
Nintendo Games Secrets Greatest Tips
Sega Genesis Secrets, Volumes 1, 2, 3, 4, and 5
Sega Genesis Games Secrets Greatest Tips
Official Sega Genesis Power Tips Book, 2nd Edition (in full color!)
TurboGrafx–16 and TurboExpress Games Secrets, Volumes 1 and 2
The Legend of Zelda: A Link to the Past Game Secrets
Super Star Wars Official Game Secrets
Super Empire Strikes Back Official Game Secrets
Super Battletoads Official Game Secrets
Secret of Mana: The Official Strategy Guide

COMPUTER GAME BOOKS

SimEarth: The Official Strategy Guide
Harpoon Battlebook: The Official Strategy Guide
The Official Lucasfilm Games Air Combat Strategies Book
Sid Meier's Civilization, or Rome on 640K a Day
Wing Commander I and II: The Ultimate Strategy Guide
Ultima: The Avatar Adventures
Ultima VII and Underworld: More Avatar Adventures
A-Train: The Official Strategy Guide
Dynamix Great War Planes: The Ultimate Strategy Guide
Gunship 2000: The Official Strategy Guide
Falcon 3: The Official Combat Strategy Book (with disk)
SimLife: The Official Strategy Guide
Stunt Island: The Official Strategy Guide
Prince of Persia: The Official Strategy Guide
X-Wing: The Official Strategy Guide
Lemmings: The Official Companion
The 7th Guest: The Official Strategy Guide

How to Order:

Quantity discounts are available from the publisher, Prima Publishing, P.O. Box 1260BK, Rocklin, CA 95677; fax #(916) 632-4405. On your letterhead include information concerning the intended use of the books and the number of books you wish to purchase. Turn to the back of the book for more information.

Myst

Official Strategy Guide

Rick Barba

&

Rusel DeMaria

P Prima Publishing
P.O. Box 1260BK
Rocklin, CA 95677
(916) -632-4400

Executive Editor: Roger Stewart
Managing Editor: Neweleen Trebnik
Creative Director, Secrets of the Games: Rusel DeMaria
Project Editor: Becky Freeman
Design and Layouts: Mychelle Brazenor (Knight), Rusel DeMaria
Cover Design: The Dunlavey Studio
Special Image Processing: Ocean Quigley
Special thanks to Matt O'Hara at Brøderbund, and also to Laurie Strand, Ken Goldstein, Jessica Switzer and Bruce Freiedricks.

Created by DeMaria Studio for
Prima Publishing, Rocklin, CA

ISBN 1-55958-480-7

Library of Congress Number: 93-86199

95 96 97 98 RRD 20 19 18 17 16 15 14 13 12 11 10

Printed in the United States of America

Contents

Introduction vi

The Myst Journal

1. Myst Island 1

2. The Library 27

3. The Selenitic Age 43

4. The Stoneship Age 61

5. The Mechanical Age 79

6. The Channelwood Age 91

7. The Endgame 111

Myst Quick Guide

Myst Quick Guide 116

Introduction:

How to Use This Book

Since you're reading this, we can only assume that you're hopelessly mired in Myst.

Don't be ashamed. It happens. Maybe you're obsessed with the fireplace door. What's it do? Is that liquid mercury or what? Maybe you have existential dreams about tree-climbing in Channelwood — up, down, up, down, nothing happens, no progress, nada. Or maybe your personal Myst nightmare involves aimless maze-running in the bowels of the Selenitic Age.

But you're stuck. Frustrated. Angry, maybe. You want to tell the observation tower to go rotate itself.

Thank god you found us.

OK, here's how it works:

The first part of this book, the Myst Journal, leads you "softly" through the game. It features an Everyman sort of narrator who chronicles his attempt to unravel the Myst mystery. His approach is observational — that is, he explores Myst, noting items of interest and leading you toward general strategies. So you can read the various sections of the Myst Journal for hints if you don't necessarily want puzzle solutions right away. Note, however, that the journalist will always give you detailed solutions sooner or later.

The second part of this books is called the Quick Guide to Myst. It's a straightforward, no-frills "walkthough." It gives you step-by-step instructions for completing the game. Of course, Myst is not strictly linear in structure; you can visit the four Ages in any order you wish. So remember that the Quick Guide is but one of many ways to complete the game.

Those of you familiar with strategy guides for games like Myst will find this book's approach familiar. But even if you've never consulted a strategy guide before, we think you'll find our format extremely easy to use.

Myst
Journal

MYST JOURNAL

Here I sit, on this dock. Seagulls. Water slapping at moorings. Like an Otis Redding tune. Beyond melancholy. I'm not exactly sure how to begin this journal. Maybe I should open with a joke. Or better, a picture. Worth a thousand words.

Beautiful, isn't it? It's from a book. I took the photo myself. If it looks slightly blurred, well, that's because it was moving when I shot it. Not the book. Not the camera. The picture. The picture was moving. This book — what can I say? Where do I start?

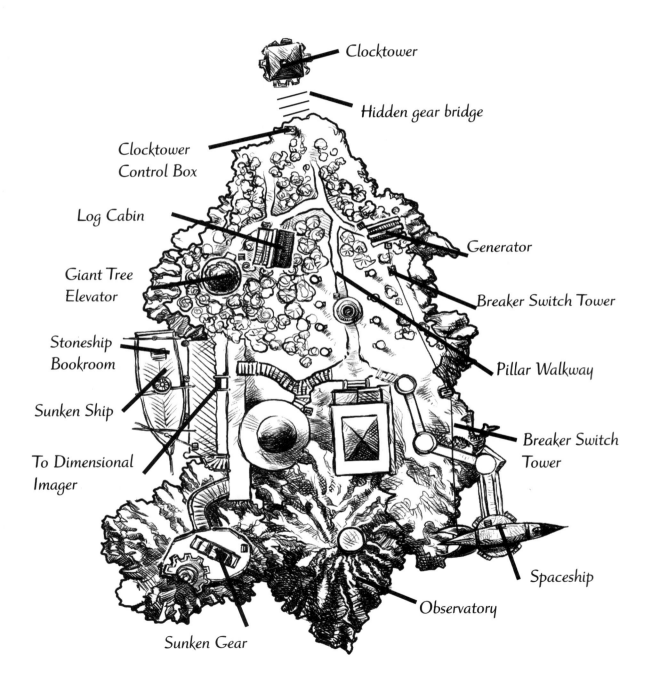

Clocktower

Hidden gear bridge

Clocktower
Control Box

Log Cabin

Generator

Giant Tree
Elevator

Breaker Switch Tower

Stoneship
Bookroom

Pillar Walkway

Sunken Ship

Breaker Switch
Tower

To Dimensional
Imager

Spaceship

Observatory

Sunken Gear

1. Myst Island

At the beginning, I suppose.

Although that may not be possible yet. Because right now, beginning, middle, and end are largely obscured in Myst.

    So I'll start at my beginning.

    I won't bore you with personal back story. What's more to the point is how I got on this dock. One moment I'm a guy in the San Francisco public library. Deep in the stacks, digging for books on photography. Next thing I know, I'm wandering a mythical island.

    Fortunately, I have a camera. Carrying case, plenty of film. If I couldn't document this place, nobody would believe it.

    But back to the setup. Like I said, I got this new instamatic. I wanted to use it in an artful way. So I hit the library. There I am, doing a little research when I come across this dusty, battered old book. I like books — OK, I'm a book guy, I admit it — so I pull it out.

    I opened it, started reading.

It was a journal. Handwritten! With meticulous care, the writer described an island — mythical, I assumed — from which travelers could embark on journeys to fantastic worlds. "Ages," they were called. I read obsessively to the very last page, which framed a dark illustration.

I looked closer.

At first it seemed a simple line drawing — dark background etched with a few darker lines. But suddenly, the lines seemed to waver, then move. I fumbled for my camera. The illustration was coming alive! It panned up to a blue horizon. Fortunately, I had film loaded. I snapped pictures just as the book began its aerial approach to an island that looked to be the very one described earlier in the journal.

The flight ended with a breathtaking landing on a dock.

Then something amazing happened.

I wanted one last good shot. But the page, I noticed, was wrinkled. I tucked the camera in its case, reached out to smooth the page. My palm touched the living image.

Everything went black.

When consciousness returned, I was standing on that very dock. I had, in essence — perhaps in actuality — entered the book. And for the last several hours, I've been exploring the very place I'd just spent hours reading about in the library. Now, as I sit here watching gulls, it seems increasingly important that I keep a faithful journal of this experience.

Let me start with my arrival.

The Dock

I stood there, dumbfounded.

To my right, the crow's nest of a sunken ship rose from the water. To my left, a hill led up to a pair of Greek-looking structures, lots of pillars. Behind me rose a wooded promontory. A hulking brick structure was vaguely visible behind the trees.

I was amazed at how well-manicured these grounds were, how well-kept the dock and buildings looked. But something felt odd. It felt lonely. Sounds of water and wind only accentuated that feeling.

As I gazed up at the solid, classical architecture of the buildings rising to my left, I noticed the grooved outline of an entry below the retaining wall.

The Dimensional Imager

It was an entry passage, alright. And when I reached out to touch it, it slid open with a neat hiss.

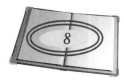

A long passageway led down stairs to an open chamber. In the center sat a bubbling vat. Witches and warlocks? But when I pressed the button, the water disappeared — illusion! Beneath, some sort of mechanism. Pressing the button again merely brought back the turbulent liquid illusion.

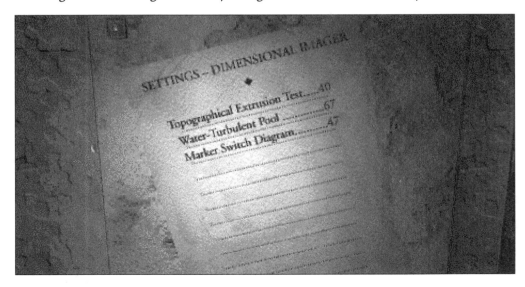

SETTINGS - DIMENSIONAL IMAGER

Topographical Extrusion Test.....40
Water-Turbulent Pool 67
Marker Switch Diagram..........47

I turned to leave. There, on the wall, was a metal plaque embossed with an image of a parchment page. I looked closer. Three different settings were etched on it:

Dimensional imager! That explains the illusory cauldron. A small green button glowed above the chart to the left. When I pressed it, the plaque slid up, revealing a hidden control panel with arrow controls for entering a two-digit number. Currently entered: 67. Of course: The "water-turbulent pool" listed on the plaque.

I entered 40, then pressed the red activation button, returned to the imager, and pressed its button as well. A stunning 3-D image of the island rose and spun on the imager's surface. Amazing. Finally, I entered 47 on the control panel. This time the imager produced a spinning "Marker Switch" — a wooden podium on a marble base, with a large-handled switch at the top.

I'd seen one of these "Marker Switches" at the base of the stairs leading up from the dock. It must be important — it certainly looks important. I decided to check it out.

Here are the three images:

The Marker Switch

I exited the Dimensional Imager chamber, then walked toward a path leading ahead to a giant gear-like object sitting atop an outcropping of rock. At the foot of the stairs sat the Marker Switch. I examined it carefully — then, on a whim, I flipped it up. It clicked, but nothing happened.

From there I went up the stairs to the base of a round, solid building. Marble. I'm no architect, but I had to admire the classic beauty of this structure. To my left, more stairs, the ones leading up to front entrances of the buildings. But I decided to go right first, up the curving stairway.

At the top sat what looked to be a huge, sunken gear.

Sunken Gear

As I approached the giant gear, I saw that another Marker Switch sat at its base. Again, I flipped up the switch. Again, nothing. The huge gear sat motionless, not a sound.

I did a quick survey. To my left, across a ravine, sat the large dome-topped rotunda. To its right, a central peak rose sharply, towering over the island. At its top squatted some kind of cylindrical structure — a watchtower? Some sort of observatory perhaps?

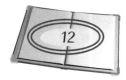

Didn't see any telescope slot though. Nor any discernible pathway up.

Catherine's Note

Catherine,
I've left for you a message of utmost importance in our fore-chamber beside the dock. Enter the number of Marker Switches on this island into the imager to retrieve the message.
Yours,
Atrus

Here's the note:

I went back down, then around the rotunda. As I moved up the path, I found a crumpled sheet of paper. Remarkably intact. As if tossed down minutes before. I looked around. Nothing moving. Not a sound. Maybe ghosts live here. Maybe I exist in the wrong dimension.

Atrus? Catherine? Interesting. I knew about the fore-chamber, the imager. And I'd seen two of these Marker Switches already. From now on I'd be sure to note each new one I found, and where I found it.

I'd like to see that message.

The Plantarium

Next, I came to the entrance of the rotunda. Finely dappled gray marble, wooden door, some sort of ornate, gilded doorplate. To its left, another Marker Switch, number three now. Flipped it up again. Wondered what the heck I was doing.

The door was heavy, solid oak, but it opened easily enough. Inside: lit up, some sort of chair in the center of the room. This thing was a real

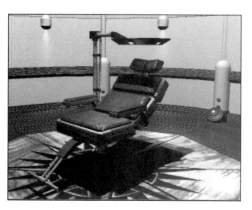

specimen. Deep-hued, full-grain leather. Real craftsmanship. Like everything else on the island.

Then I noticed something glowing blue just right of the doorway. Kind of big for just a light switch. I gave it a try, looked up: Stars. A planetarium! It was a sight. Gorgeous.

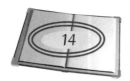

I went back to the chair and sat in it. Above, I noticed some sort of amazing control panel. I pulled it down, examined it — readouts for date, time, and what seemed to be an activation button. A constellation of stars dotted the view screen.

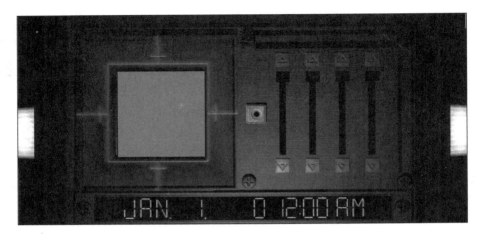

I was very tempted to make some random entries to see what happened. So I entered my birthday. The button started flashing with the first entry. I pushed it. The viewscreen panned across the starfield, centered on another constellation. Some kind of star charting device! I could play with this for hours if there wasn't so much left to be explored. I moved the panel back up into place.

I left the room and reluctantly shut the door.

The Library

At the walkway, I went right. Up ahead sat a truly impressive, Parthenon-style columned structure with an open door. I remembered it from the Myst book's flyover approach. In fact, I'd snapped a photo:

I stepped into a huge, octagonal room. Everything was burnished wood, made with godlike craftsmanship. The detail was astounding. Straight ahead, the centerpiece of the room — a three-tiered bookshelf.

A library. I thought of the Myst book that got me here. And I remembered its references to a library filled with portals to other worlds, other ages. This must be it.

I stared at the books in front of me.

Everything in me wanted to grab them, rip them open. Put my hands on the pages, read, devour. But for some reason, I didn't. Something told me this place was the beating heart of Myst. It would be better to culminate my exploration of the island here.

I contented myself with a quick survey. Paintings. A fireplace. A map. Two large books, blue and red, on display.

Then I left.

THE MYSTERY CRAFT

Outside, on the far side of the library, sat an odd blimplike craft. Parked at the end of a meticulously constructed platform. I approached. Wind whistling. To be honest, it looked like a big lawn dart. Almost humorous. Does it fly? Or some sort of submersible?

I noticed that a power line runs right to it.

The door wouldn't open. So I flipped up another another Marker Switch, number four. Then I headed back to the path . . . on the way, I noticed a ladder leading up the brick tower that supports the power line.

Without thinking, I climbed it. At the top, a switch. Looks like some kind of circuit breaker. No use tripping it, though. No power humming in the wires. No wonder the craft's door won't open.

PILLAR WALKWAY

I left the platform and headed down a path that ran between a column of pillars. Ahead, a small basin. Bird bath? But when I looked in, I saw a sunken miniature replica of the boat by the dock — exposed crow's nest and all!

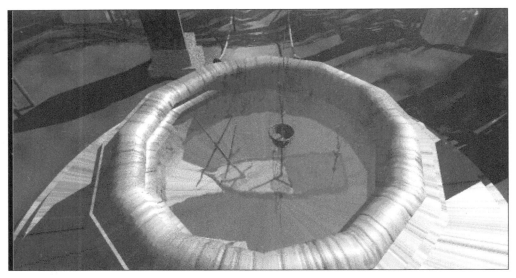

Just behind and left of the basin was another marker switch — number five now — which I flipped up. Dead ahead, in the distance, I could see a large clock tower.

Before moving farther on, I examined the odd assortment of pillars and markers lining the path. At the base of the first pillar on the left was a marker inscribed with a bird icon. Whenever my hand got near it, it hummed and turned crimson. Should I touch it? Why not. When I did, it clicked, and the inscription turned green. I touched it again, and it turned back to red.

All the other markers exhibit the same phenomenon.

Here's a list of the marker inscriptions, listed in order, on each side as they lead away from the library:

LEFT	RIGHT
bird	eye
cross	serpent
leaf	insect
arrow	anchor

As I walked along the markers on the right side, I noticed a power line (the one connected to the "dart" craft) strung along a series of brick supports running parallel to the path. They skirt the cliff's edge. Ending at a squat-looking brick building.

I took a few steps down the path. Twin monarch butterflies flew past — beautiful, idyllic. Then I went right, to the cliff's edge. Worked my way around the last brick tower.

A ladder ran to the tower's top. I climbed it, and, to no surprise, found another circuit breaker trip switch there.

GENERATOR

I climbed back down and carefully worked my way back around to the front of the brick building. Since the power lines ended here, I assumed the structure housed a generator plant of some sort. Before entering, though, I flipped up the Marker Switch just to the left of the entrance.
Sixth one so far. Still, I wish I knew what I was doing.

   I stepped through the brick entry, down winding stairs. Dank, musty, and extremely eerie. At the bottom, a door, another blue glowing button. I pushed the button, the door hissed open, and I entered a small control room.

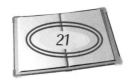
The control panel is simply laid out — a pair of gauges, two rows of buttons. The room's window overlooks a cavernous plant, with rows of huge generators stretching off into the darkness.

I fought the urge to just mess around. Instead, I turned to go. As I left, I discovered a chart tacked to the wall just to the right of the door:

Spaceship! Could that be what I saw next to the Library? The schematic drawing of generator switches obviously referred to the two rows of buttons on the control panel behind me.

I hurried back upstairs.

The fresh air felt good in my lungs. I turned right, down the path toward the clocktower.

THE CLOCKTOWER

As I got closer, I could see that the clocktower was actually offshore. It sits on a gearshaped platform. Apparently gears are real big in the decorating scheme around here. The face read 12 o'clock, with a large door carved below, in the base. I could also see another Marker Switch (number seven, I noted) to the left of the door.

On the shore, I found some kind of control box. Two wheels and a red button. Each turn of the large wheel moved the clock's big hand forward an increment of five minutes. Each turn of the small wheel moved the clock's small hand forward an increment of one hour.

I pushed the button. Nothing happened.

LOG CABIN

I turned and headed back toward the Library.

As I trudged up the bucolic path, I caught a glimpse of something, nearly hidden by foliage, to my right. There, tucked amongst the trees, sat a rustic log cabin. Easy to miss. And just to the right of the front door sat Marker Switch number eight — which, as always, I flipped up.

I opened the creaky door, entered. Straight ahead hunkered what appeared to be a gas furnace with a hydraulic pressure gauge on the front. A large red wheel to the right. A valve? To the left, an illustration of a tree trunk rising from a brick platform.

I pulled down on the right side of the gearwheel, turning it clockwise. A low hiss began, then grew louder. The smell of gas became unmistakable. The more I turned the wheel, the louder the hissing grew. But I could see no flame in the furnace box below the pressure compartment. Looking closer, I noticed a pilot light box — unlit.

Anybody got a match? Not me.

I quickly turned the gearwheel counterclockwise, shutting off the gas. Maybe if I find a source of flame on this island, I'll return and give that pilot light a try. I turned back. Just right of the door, a safe in the wall. Handle and three number combination lock.

THE GIANT TREE

Just for fun, I thought I'd stroll around in the woods behind the cabin before heading back to the Library. I slipped between the first couple of trees to the right of the door, then rounded the cabin. To my surprise, I found myself facing the same tree and platform depicted in the illustration next to the furnace inside.

This tree was huge. It towered far above the others. I remembered it from the Myst book flyover. But standing at its base, looking up, was an almost religious experience.

I examined it carefully, but it appeared to simply be a tree in a platform. Why? Maybe a place of worship for some kind of radical environmentalist cult. Chuckling at my third-rate humor, I returned to the path, walked back to the dock, and sat down to start this journal.

And that's where I am now.

At this point it strikes me — I think I've found all the visible Marker Switches on this island. Eight in all. Maybe more hidden, but I want to try this number in the Dimensional Imager. Maybe I'll get Atrus's message to Catherine now.

THE DOCK FORECHAMBER

I entered "08" in the imager control panel, and it worked! The message was pretty unsettling, though. A man appeared, speaking (as in the note) to his beloved wife, Catherine. So this is Atrus!

In the message he says he has to leave quickly, something terrible has happened. Someone has destroyed most of his books. Says in shock: "It's one

of our sons!" He suspects Achenar, but doesn't want to leap to conclusions. Atrus adds that he removed the remaining undamaged books from the library and placed them in what he calls "the places of protection."

Then he says something most intriguing: "If you've forgotten the access keys, remember the tower of rotation."

At this point it seems I've seen all I can see of the island.

Time now to return to the library — and the books that promise to enlighten me further.

2. THE LIBRARY

THE BOOKS

So, the library. It seems to hold the key to this mystery.

Heading straight for the bookshelf, I decided to be systematic about this. I started at the top, worked my way down, book by book. It was shocking. Most of the books were indeed destroyed. Horribly charred, burned beyond reclamation. Exactly as Atrus had said in his message to Catherine. But I found five that were spared.

What follows is a brief catalog of what each contains:

CHANNELWOOD AGE JOURNAL

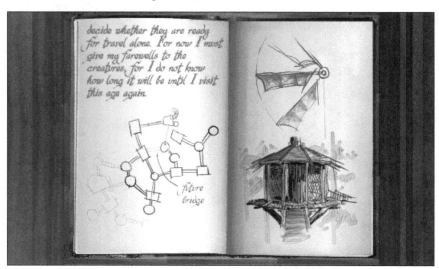

The first intact tome was the green and red book, top shelf, far left.

A journal. Same handwriting as the Myst book. The writer opens with talk of something he calls the Channelwood Age. He speaks of monkey-like people, tree-dwellers. An entire tree village, in fact. Described as rising from the ocean itself.

This journal also mentioned his wife Catherine, his sons Sirrus and Achenar. Must be Atrus. Pages of fascinating discussion of the age — its history, legends, and so on.

It ends with this diagram of what looks like a community of huts connected by walkways or bridges. Is this the tree village?

STONESHIP AGE JOURNAL

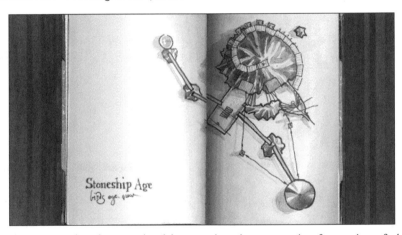

Stoneship Age
bird's eye view

The next intact book was the blue and red one at the far right of the top shelf.

It seemed at first a fairy tale. Story of three boys, Emmit, Branch and Will — but then the narrator, Atrus, enters the story, speaking of a "newly created age" and something called The Art. Various sketches of gadgets: a blinking light, a submersible lamp. Also, there is talk of building a lighthouse, powering up a generator, and the like.

Then this map-like overview labeled "Stoneship Age - bird's eye view":

The journal closes with sketches of eight major constellations that Atrus has observed. Paging through them fired a spark of recognition. Each matched one of the marker inscriptions at the base of the pillars just outside!

I took photos of all eight, hoping to catch a glimpse of them myself in the night sky of Myst.

SELENITIC AGE JOURNAL

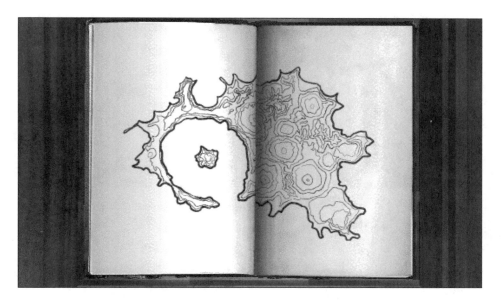

After a batch of burned books I came to the blue book tilted on the middle shelf. This one speaks of another "age" full of horrible cataclysm, meteoric fireballs, chasms, underground caverns. It also speaks of Sirrus and Achenar, left behind in Channelwood. At times the writing fades in and out, which the writer later notes.

After some sketches of valves, a radio dish and a drawing of the spaceship, I came upon something most interesting — a sketch of a keyboard with a numbered sequence of five notes. No doubt important in some way, so I snapped a photo and tucked it in my carrying case.

Finally, on the last page, this sketched map of the Selenitic island:

THE PATTERN BOOK

One of the burned books was still readable. I found it at the far right on the middle shelf. It contains some 300 different patterns of black squares on a 6 X 8 grid.

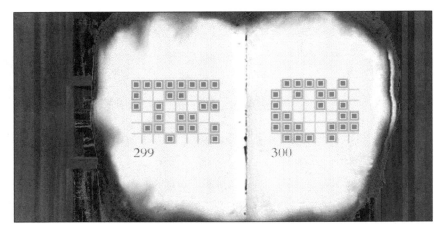

A puzzle book? Or code book, maybe. But for what? I put it back on the shelf.

MECHANICAL AGE

The last unburned book had a black cover, sat on the left side of the bottom shelf. Its subject: a Mechanical Age, a land of dark, gray skies tinged yellow by flashes of lightning. Tales of a once-beautiful city, surrounded by three hills, sinking into the sea after destruction at the hands of enemy ships. Atrus decided to provide a fortress of defense, returned with his two sons.

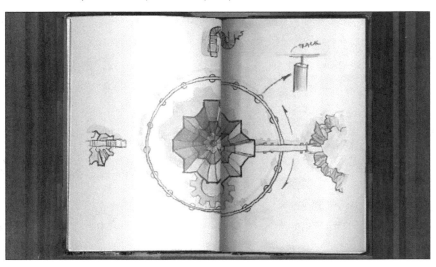

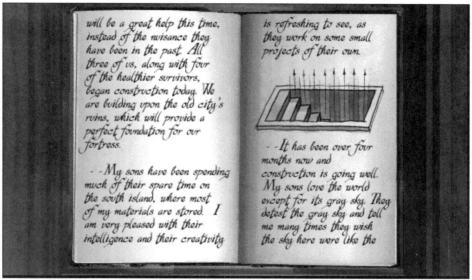

The finished structure apparently sits on the three original hills, which are now islands.

Again, sketches dot the book. One depicts a sunken stairway that can rise to a flush surface. There's also a diagram of the fortress itself. Ingenious. A track on pillars surrounds it.

THE PAINTINGS

All the other books were blackened shells. A real crime.

On either side of the bookshelf hang paintings. To the left: Stairs leading through an arch, very much

like the arches carved into the wood paneling of the room. When I looked closer, I noticed that the "stairs" appeared to be bookshelves much like the ones just to the right — and when I touched it, the painting swirled, transmogrified before my very eyes!

The picture now depicted a staircase leading into a passage:

I shook my head and stepped away. Suddenly, the actual bookshelf to the right underwent the same transformation! Behind me, the entrance to the library sealed shut at the same time.

I wanted to complete my examination of this room before exploring any secret chambers that might lie at the end of the passageway. So I went to the other painting, to the right of the bookshelf. A representation of the library's open doorway.

Again, on close examination, a swirling change. Then the bookshelf rose up to its original state, and the library door slid open.

At this point, I decided to take nothing for granted on Myst Island.

I scanned the rest of the room. Sitting apart — two books, one blue and one red. A page of matching color sat beside each.

THE BLUE BOOK

I went to the blue book first, picked up the page. It obviously belonged to the book, so I slid it in. Suddenly, the blackened illustration on the right side of the page filled with static — and came to life! It was a message. A young man, obviously distressed, suddenly looked up at me and called out, "Sirrus? Is that you?"

When he realized I was a stranger, he began imploring me to "bring the blue pages." More heavy static marred the transmission, but I could make out a phrase or two — something about "forever and ever" and repeated demands for these blue pages.

THE RED BOOK

The red book's message was similar. Another young man struggling to see and hear me. He began demanding the red pages — thought he said something like "I am Sirrus." The son of whom Atrus spoke?

Honestly can't say I liked his attitude any more than the other guy's. Kind of arrogant, curt. But then I thought, Maybe I'd be desperate and impatient if I was living in a book too.

And then I thought: Hey. I am living in a book.

THE FIREPLACE

Next, I examined the fireplace.

Seemed normal enough, until I turned around to get out. A small red switch nestled, nearly hidden, to the left of the opening. When I pressed it, a door dropped shut in front of me.

In a panic, I reached out to push the door open — and a small square indentation literally "grew" from the spot I touched! The surface felt cold and yielding, like mercury. I touched it again and again, watching the squares leap to life, forming a pattern.

Suddenly, I remembered the Pattern Book on the center bookshelf. I checked the door. Squares. Six by eight grid. Exactly. Some kind of pattern access code. But access to what?

I thought of entering each of the 300 patterns, trial and error. Then I thought better.

When I pushed the red button again, the squares disappeared and the door jerked open with a pneumatic hiss.

THE OBSERVATORY

I was ready now to explore behind the bookshelf.

I went back to the bookshelf painting, and touched it. Then stepped back as the secret passageway re-opened. I followed the twisting corridor until I reached an open chamber.

There sat an elevator.

I opened its door and entered.

An indicator light above a blue button told me I was at the "Library." I shut the door and pushed the button, trusting to fate. When the car stopped moving, I opened the door. The indicator now read "Tower." Could this be the building I'd seen on the high peak overlooking the island?

Dead ahead was a metal ladder with an "open book" insignia centered on the wall behind it.

I climbed the ladder and found an observation deck with an open viewing slot. But the view was blocked by a solid granite wall. I climbed back down and peeked behind the elevator — there was another ladder on the opposite wall, this one framing a "key" insignia.

I remembered Atrus's words to Catherine on the Dimensional Imager: "If you've forgotten the access keys, then remember the tower of rotation." Does this tower rotate? If so, how?

I climbed the ladder, and again there was nothing but pure granite wall at the top. Most curious. Again, I wondered if there was some way to rotate the slot? I returned to the elevator.

And here I sit now. Staring again at the "open book" insignia on the wall. These symbols seem to suggest that the "key" to this observatory can be found in certain books.

I should return to the library.

THE MAP

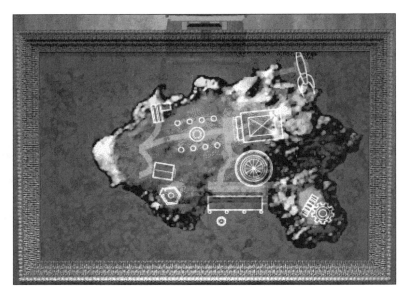

As I entered the llibrary, it struck me that there was one element of this room still unexamined — the map.

As I approached it, an illuminated overlay suddenly appeared. I looked closely. Diagrammatic line drawings of island structures! Each seemed to correspond to locations at which I'd flipped Marker Switches.

I wanted to test if the Marker Switches had anything to do with these illuminated map features. I went out and flipped off the Marker Switch by the basin. Returned, looked at the map. Sure enough, no diagram for that area. I went back out, switched it on again. At last, I knew. The switches activate some sort of holographic mapping grid.

Looking closer, I noticed that the icon for the observation tower behind the library was flashing. As I reached out to touch the flashing concentric circles, a beam of light shot from it and began to sweep in an arc around the map. I noticed that the beam stopped its sweep when I withdrew my hand. Then the words "Tower Rotation" flashed and I heard a powerful mechanical rumbling — the real observation tower was turning!

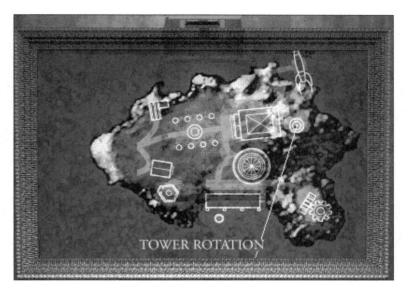

TOWER ROTATION

I reached out again, and watched the beam turned red as it passed over each of the marker switch locations. I decided to hold on the observatory until the beam rotated and turned red over the the object I'd found most interesting thus far — the spaceship at the upper-right of the map.

I listened to the "tower rotation" again, then hurried back to the observatory.

Sure enough, the viewing slot revealed the spaceship. But what did that show me? I decided to check the opposite ladder (the one with the "key" insignia).

This time, at the top, a gleaming metallic plaque had been revealed, engraved with this:

I immediately thought of the "power to spaceship" gauge in the cave beneath the brick power house, and those two rows of generator switches. I jumped in the elevator and returned to the library. Then I used the door painting again to reopen the front entry.

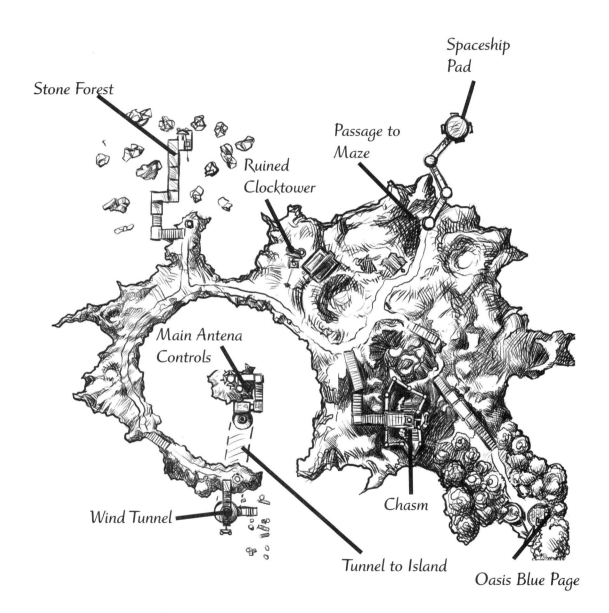

Stone Forest

Spaceship Pad

Ruined Clocktower

Passage to Maze

Main Antena Controls

Wind Tunnel

Chasm

Tunnel to Island

Oasis Blue Page

3. SELENITIC AGE

SPACESHIP ACTIVATION

I went down the path and into the generator cave, went to the control panel, looking to power up the generators to 59 watts. I went down the left row, pushing buttons, jotting down voltage increases of each — 10, 7, 8, 16, 5 — now I was up to 46. I went down the second row — 1, 2, 22 — oops, that put me at 71, and the right gauge shut down to zero!

Must have tripped the breaker switches. I shut down all generators.

I decided to throw the circuit breaker switch just outside. Before leaving, though, I decided to push the last two generator buttons, noting the voltage of each — 19 and 9. I realized now that I'd have to come up with exactly 59 volts, or I'd trip the breaker again.

As I climbed the stairs I did some quick mental addition, trying to find combinations that worked. When I got to top of the tower, I discovered that the switch wasn't tripped there. I proceeded to the other breaker tower I'd seen on the path to the spaceship, climbed it, threw that switch.

Back at the generator room, I tried my combination:

LEFT ROW
one (10v)
three (18v)

RIGHT ROW
three (22v)
four (19v)

As I headed back to spaceship, I could hear the power humming in the wires. This time the ship's door slid neatly open when I touched it, and I stepped in.

To the left was an odd control device with sliders that traversed a scale of musical notes when moved up or down. A large handle, which appeared to be some sort of power-on switch, triggered the note sequence set by the slider positions. I tried a few combinations, but nothing happened.

Then I remembered the five-note sequence sketched in the Selenitic journal in the library. Five notes. Five slider bars. A musical code! Clever. I was glad I'd photographed it.

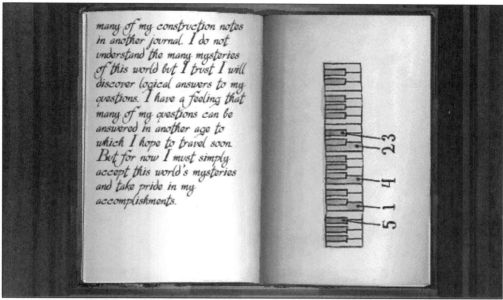

many of my construction notes in another journal. I do not understand the many mysteries of this world but I trust I will discover logical answers to my questions. I have a feeling that many of my questions can be answered in another age to which I hope to travel soon. But for now I must simply accept this world's mysteries and take pride in my accomplishments.

A beautiful harpsichord gleamed at the other end of the ship. I went to it, fingered the first note in the sequence, then hurried back to the tuner. It took a couple trips back to the harpsichord (and a good tonal ear) to get the proper code loaded on the sliders.

Here's what it looked like when I got it right:

I pulled the handle, and the portal-like viewscreen came alive with a floating book. By this time I knew what to do. Placing my hand on the portal, I watched it transform into a flyby of a desolate-looking island. Then again, all went black — signalling my arrival in the Selenitic Age.

SELENITIC AGE

I am sitting in a tiny oasis on one of the most godforsaken places I have ever seen. Let me bring this up-to-date.

The "flight," if you can call it that, was instantaneous. On arrival, I stepped out of the ship. Water lapping. Gentle roar of surf. The landing platform ran out to the sea. I walked down a ramp. Up ahead — a barren, lifeless world. Burned out. The first structure I came to was small, jutting out from the rock face. Some kind of portal. Its door was sealed shut.

I remembered the underground caverns mentioned in the Selenitic journal. Could this be a passage to them?

But the door was locked by another five-sound code, keyed again by slider bars. I slid a bar up and down a few times, listening. Where to find this sequence? I began to explore.

CHASM

I saw a brick stairway ahead, left of the road. Behind that, some kind of tower rose in the mist, with what looked like a radar-antenna at the top. I

followed the stairs to the base of the tower, a brick podium. On it, a red button was installed beneath a golden icon symbol that appeared to depict wind or heat rising from a jagged opening.

When I looked down on either side of the platform, I understood the meaning of the icon.

This must be the massive chasm that Atrus spoke of in his Selenitic journal. The yawning thing drops straight down to reveal glowing molten rock. Burning gases rise from the depths. I could feel the heat.

When I pushed the red button, and the chasm etching suddenly glowed. What this meant, I had no idea. Off to the left, suspended from a cable, hung some kind of gadget with a red tip. Some sort of a detection device? In fact, it looked like a microphone.

If so, what might it be recording? All I could hear was the fiery roar of the chasm below. And then it hit me. This sound: I'd heard it before. Back at the portal.

The slider bar sound code!

OASIS

I came back down the stairs. I glanced right: What a wasteland. The portal building sat there, enshrouded in a smoky mist. Then I noticed a small worn path branching off to the right.

I followed it. It led to more brick stairs, running behind the chasm. Then I saw trees. Life! A bit further, and suddenly I found myself in midst of lush vegetation. I heard running water. An oasis on this blackened island. The oasis where I sit now, writing these words.

To the right, as I approached, I saw a well of fresh water flowing through a sluice gate, then down the hill. Above it, another red-tipped device. Took a good close look. It must be a microphone.

I thought about sound. The portal door code. I listened to the peaceful babble of the water.

To the left sat another podium. Another button, another icon — this one of water dripping. I pushed the button. To the left, a blue page fluttered precariously on a small platform. I took it.

RUINED CLOCKTOWER

I returned to the main path, turned left. Past the stairs to the chasm. Straight ahead lay the charred ruins of a clocktower, still ticking and tolling, though somewhat erratically. Again, I recognized the sound from the slider bar code on the portal door.

At the tower's base lay another red button and icon, this time of a clock. I pushed the button and moved on down the path.

STONE FOREST

I had to traverse a jagged narrow peninsula to another Y-branch, where I turned right. The footing was getting precarious, but thankfully, I found more brick stairs. Ahead, rising up out of the ocean mist, was a breathtaking sight. Multicolor columns of rock or crystal jutting up from the water. Towering, diamond-like configurations.

It was like a stone forest.

But almost more spectacular was the sound. The wind was playing music in the rock towers. I can only describe the sound as . . . tubular. And again, familiar.

I followed a narrow brick passageway leading out to a small platform that sat in the midst of the rock formations. A brick column rose from it, suspending another antenna and microphone. At its base was another podium, complete with red button and a columnar icon.

Sitting atop the podium was a red page.

I took the page, and something odd happened — the blue page disintegrated in my hand! I pushed the red button and headed back to the Y-branch in the peninsula path.

Just out of curiousity, I returned to the oasis. There sat the blue page, just as it was when I first saw it. Apparently, only one page can be carried at a time. Maybe I can return for this one later.

Then again, maybe not.

WIND TUNNEL

I returned to the Y-branch in the peninsula. Took the left fork this time. As I moved along, I glanced to my left at the small island out in the lagoon. Ahead, more brick stairs, then another podium next to a broken, rotting pier. A ladder led down a well-like hole. Wind whistled out. It was the wind tunnel sound from the portal slider bar.

I pushed the red button on the podium. Then I took a deep breath — and climbed down.

MAIN ANTENNA CONTROLS

At the bottom of the ladder I found a switch that turned on a light. I moved through the tunnel to a second ladder, and climbed up. When I emerged I could see I'd reached that small island in the lagoon.

I followed the path to another podium. This one looked sealed shut by big sheet metal doors. But they swung open easily, revealing a control panel with a video display, two direction arrow buttons, a 360-degree direction indicator, and five icon buttons that matched the five I'd seen at button locations throughout the island. There was also a summation icon button at the bottom. When I pushed it, it merely played a sequence of five sounds, all the same. I guessed that I had to load the five sounds somehow before the summation button would show me the proper sequence for the portal code.

I clicked on the first icon button, the one that matched the oasis icon. The camera view changed, and the direction indicator went to 0 degrees. When I clicked the right directional button, the camera view began to swing right and the indicator started counting up, displaying the direction in degrees that I was seeing in the viewer.

I kept swinging the camera right, getting nothing but static — until I got to 148.5 degrees. At that point the right arrow began flashing, and I could hear the faint sound of water — the oasis. I kept the view swivelling right a few tenths of a degree at a time. Finally, at 153.4, the static disappeared, and the running water sound from the oasis locked in.

Obviously, the microphones I'd seen were broadcasting sounds from their various locations to this receiver tower through the large antennae arrayed above. I pressed the summation button again; again, the panel played five segments of sound. But this time the oasis sound was the second in the sequence! And its degree setting, 153.4, appeared in the direction indicator while the sound played. Now, apparently, I needed to lock in the other four sounds.

As I did this, I noticed that whenever I got within five degrees of the proper direction on either side, the appropriate arrow flashed to show which direction to proceed.

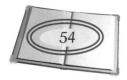

Here are photos showing each icon locked in to the proper directional bearing:

Stone Forest Setting

Oasis Setting

Windtunnel Setting

Chasm Setting

Once I'd gotten all these, I pressed the button, and the controller played back the five sounds in this sequence:

Stone Forest

Oasis

Windtunnel

Chasm

Clock

I knew this must be the portal door code. I listened to the

Clock Setting

sequence several times, memorizing the sounds. Then I returned to oasis to rest and bring this journal up-to-date.

Next stop: The portal building.

ELEVATOR

The sound code worked like a charm.

Back at the portal building, I entered the sequence in the slider mechanism, pushed the button, and the door opened. Here's a photo of the proper slider alignment:

I followed a long metallic passageway to a large open chamber in which sat a remarkable pod-like car on a rail track.

I pressed the blue entry button and the doors slid open. When I entered, the doors snapped shut behind me. I sat in the pilot's chair of what turned out to be some sort of Mazerunner.

THE MAZE

Once aboard, I examined the control panel in front of me. It looked simple enough.

I pushed the FORWARD button, watched as the runner lowered onto a single-rail track. Then I heard a small bell sound — bing. After a lot of trial and error, I learned it was a directional cue, tied to sounds just like everything else in this age.

Two other things I learned. If I missed the sound the first time, I found I could repeat it by simply pressing the red flashing button at the left. And when I got lost or misguided, I found that pressing BACKTRACK took me back towards my last correct position in the maze.

Here are the directional sound cues:

N	small bell	(bing)
W	bird sound	(twrrreee)
E	airbrake	(fssss)
S	bell clank	

NE, NW, SE, SW combine the sounds of two directions

It took a while, but I got out. Here's the sequence of directions that I followed to exit the maze: N, W, N, E, E, S, S, W, SW, W, NW, NE, N, SE and out.

And now I sit here holding the Myst book again.

After arriving, I exited the Mazerunner, followed more metallic corridors to another chamber, and there it sat. I have it open to the last page — which, as always, is alive and swirling. I recognize the picture as the ceiling of the library back on Myst Island.

I hesitate — then I reach out my hand.

BACK TO MYST ISLAND

The experience was the same. My palm touched the page — and then blackness.

But this time when I awoke, I found myself lying on the floor of the library, staring up at the ceiling. Funny I hadn't really noticed it before. Stunningly beautiful.

Through all of these journeys, I've managed to hang onto my carrying case. I grabbed my camera:

Then I went directly to the red book. I inserted the red page ... and the plot, as they say, began to thicken considerably.

RED PAGE #2

The young man, I have learned for certain, is indeed Sirrus, one of the two sons of whom Atrus speaks in his journals. I also feel certain that the one in the blue book is his brother Achenar. Sirrus welcomed my return, thanked me for the red page.

The static wasn't as bad as before, but I still found it hard to understand most of his message. He implored me to bring more red pages. Most

insistent. I caught bits and pieces of some odd, disturbing statements: "I am Sirrus ... my brother is guilty ... and I wrongfully imprisoned."

Imprisoned? I remember Atrus on the Dimensional Imager, agonizing that his library had been destroyed by one of his sons. And didn't he say he suspected Achenar?

Clearly, I need to know more.

So I've decided to take a chance. I will go back and retrieve the blue page from the Selenitic age as well.

BLUE PAGE #2

The return to the Selenitic Age and retrieval of the page was surprisingly swift. All the codes were already in place, so I moved quickly — spaceship, oasis, blue page, portal, Mazerunner, back through the maze to the Myst book, then back here to the library again.

It was worth it. I put the page in the blue book. Achenar seems crazy — giggling, demanding his blue pages. He said, "Don't trust my brother, I beg you ... an egotistical fool, and a liar!" Like Sirrus, he claims he is wrongfully imprisoned. His anger spurts to the surface wildly. Final statement was quite disconcerting: "I will have my retribution!"

I will go to the map next. Try more tower rotation, look for means of travel to other ages.

But first, I need rest.

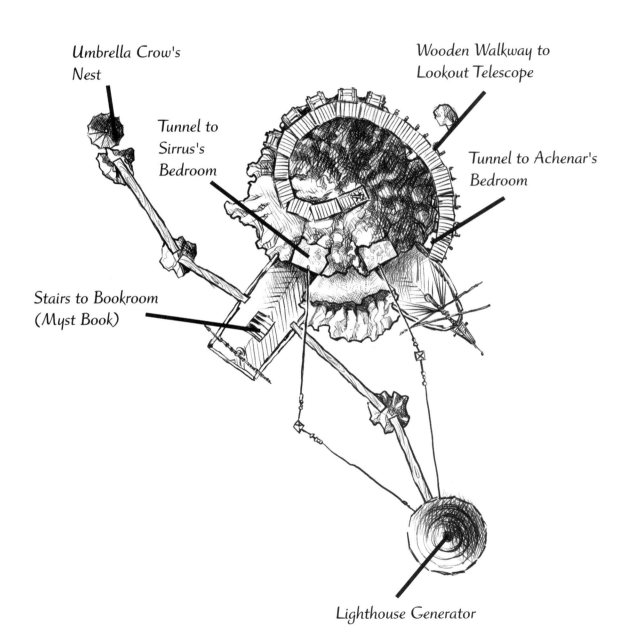

Umbrella Crow's
Nest

Tunnel to
Sirrus's
Bedroom

Wooden Walkway to
Lookout Telescope

Tunnel to Achenar's
Bedroom

Stairs to Bookroom
(Myst Book)

Lighthouse Generator

4. STONESHIP AGE

THE STAR CHARTS

At the map, I thought of the Stoneship Age journal and its reference to some sort of experiment with a ship gone awry. I manipulated the tower rotation until the beam shone red on the marker at the dock.

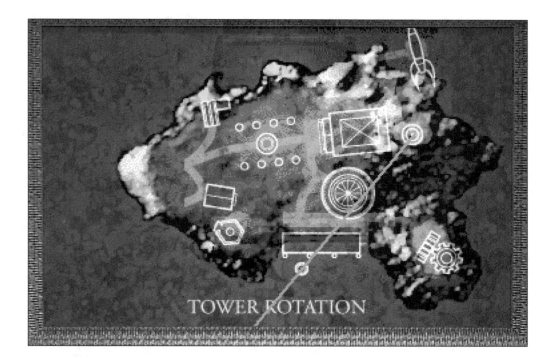

Then I opened the passage behind the bookshelf and rode up to the observatory. I went immediately to the "key" ladder behind the elevator and climbed to the top. A new plaque was uncovered, displaying three moments in time.

I took this photo of it:

 I remembered my frivolous birthdate experiment earlier. These three dates looked ripe for star plotting. I headed straight for the planetarium.

 Turned off the lights, sat in the chair, pulled down the display panel. I used the slider bars to plug-in the first date: October 11, 1984, 10:04 AM. Then I pressed the flashing button. A star constellation appeared on the viewscreen.

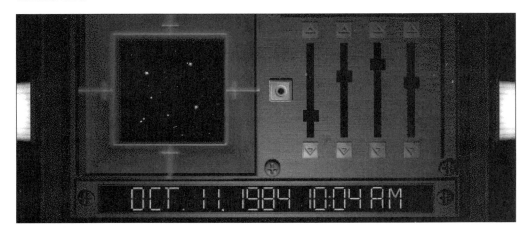

I opened my photo packet and found the shots I'd taken of the constellations sketched in the Stoneship Age book.

There it was: The Leaf.

Then I repeated the process for the other two dates, and I got the Snake and the Insect constellations . . .

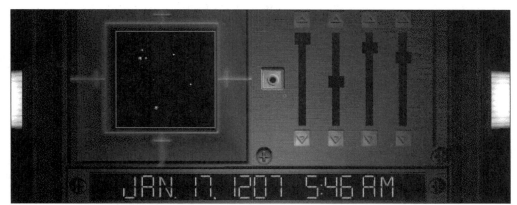

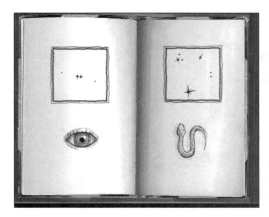

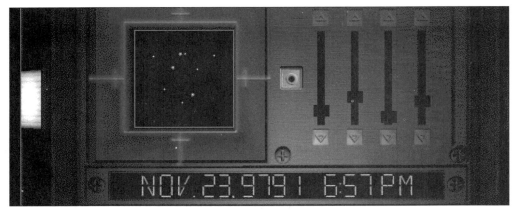

Now I sit here on the steps outside the planetarium. Three constellations. What next?

Wait. The Pillar Switches! Of course.

RAISING THE SHIP

Something amazing has happened.

But then, what part of this journey hasn't been amazing?

I went to each of the three pillar switches that match up to constellations — Leaf, Snake, and Insect — and touched each one, turning it green and apparently activating it somehow.

LEAF	third pillar on the left
SNAKE	second pillar on the right
INSECT	third pillar on the right

When I clicked the last switch, I suddenly heard a loud gurgling and rushing of water. I spun around. The small ship in the basin had risen to the surface of the water! But that still didn't account for all the sound. Then I had a rare intuitive flash, and rushed down to the dock.

The sunken boat was afloat. Tilted, but afloat. Incredible.

I went aboard, stepped into the small room below the aft deck. There, on a chair, sat another book. I thought of Atrus's term: "Places of protection." This was indeed that. I opened it and watched the flyby sequence of what I took to be the Stoneship Age.

Then I put my hand on the page ... and sank into the darkness.

STONESHIP AGE

When I emerged back into consciousness, I found myself on the deck of something that was half wooden vessel, half stone fortress. Obvious how this age got its name.

I stood on the boat's stern half, facing a dark doorway. It led into a rock wall. Inside, steps going down. But the stairwell was flooded. Same situation in the stern cabin compartment — flooded nearly to deck level.

Planks ran off the port side to an odd, umbrella-covered crow's nest. More planks ran starboard to the remains of a half-sunken lighthouse. I noted: Power lines ran from lighthouse to ship. Generator?

Stairs hewn in rock led to the other half of the ship. Another doorway into the stone fortress on this side — again, flooded. A woodplank walkway led up around the rock.

I took a couple of steps up the walkway, then looked down. Nearly passed out. I don't like heights. I decided to check out the lighthouse and crow's nest first. I'll return to this flimsy-looking climb later.

THE LIGHTHOUSE

I crossed the rickety gangplank, entered the lighthouse. Again, everything below the exterior waterline was flooded. I noticed a thick metal key chained quite sturdily to the floor. Couldn't remove it.

Thought, This is getting frustrating. Finally, I tried to climb the ladder.

But the door above my head was securely locked. I assumed (wrongly, it turns out) that the key on the floor unlocked it. Why would anyone chain a key to the floor? In any case, I had no way to get lock and key together.

So I left.

Thinking: Everything's coming to a watery dead end, it seems.

THE PUMPING STATION

Walked the plank again, this time to the crow's nest. Decided it was time to start snapping photos. Here's one:

Under the umbrella, three switches — pump switches, looked like. Which to try first? Being right-handed, I instinctively reached right. What the heck. The mechanism engaged and began to pump furiously.

I noticed water bubbling away from the lighthouse off the starboard side of the ship.

BACK TO LIGHTHOUSE

I hurried back. Sure enough, the subwater section of the lighthouse had been pumped out. I went down winding stairs. At the bottom I found nothing but a locked chest. Couldn't open it. Maybe that damn key works here instead? But again, how to get lock and key together?

I was frustrated. Ready to break something.

Then I noticed a small spigot at the lower-left of the chest, and (more out of my frustration than anything) gave it a serious twist. Water gushed out. This gave me a weird, wild idea. The chest, I figured, was now full of air — buoyant — so I closed the spigot to seal it tight.

Then I hurried upstairs, back to the pump switches, and turned the right switch off again to reflood the lighthouse. Back to the lighthouse, and there it was — the chest, floating right next to the key, which now reached it easily. I unlocked it, and found another key inside.

This key worked in the door above me.

I emerged onto a beautiful wooden observation deck, glass on all sides. Behind me sat the generator I'd suspected may be here. I cranked it up, looked at the battery pack next to it and saw I had generated maybe ten minutes worth of electricity.

I decided it was time to suck up my courage. I headed back to the rickety walkway around the rocky point.

THE LOOKOUT

Turns out the walkway is a lot more solid than it looks. Whoever built these structures knew what they were doing. At the top, I found a single lookout telescope.

I panned around awhile, until I saw a blinking light. Looked somehow familiar. Hadn't I seen something like this in a sketch? Yes. In the Stoneship journal back on Myst.

I looked closer, but could see nothing particular about it. Noting here the blinking light's position of 135 degrees, I left the telescope trained on it for future study.

SIRRUS'S BEDROOM

Now it was time to get into those tunnels.

I went back out to the crow's nest. Two other switches to try. Which? I pushed the middle one. As it fired up I went back to the boat, looked in the first tunnel there. Voila. No water.

I went down a rather long, winding set of stairs. At the bottom I found a watertight door. I pressed the button. It hissed open, revealing a well-preserved bedroom. This thing was beautiful, quite lavish. The bedroom of one of the brothers? Sirrus, I imagined. He seemed a man of exquisite (one might say snooty) demeanor ... and expensive tastes.

But perhaps, like Atrus, I'm jumping to easy conclusions.

Anyway, I wandered around. I examined a writing desk, opened its

drawer. Nothing of interest, except for syringes, needles, a few vials of drugs. Good Sirrus, a narcotics abuser? Very interesting.

I rifled the chest of drawers across the room as well. There, I found the red page in the bottom drawer.

Then it was off to the other tunnel, where I fully expected to find another bedroom. Achenar's.

ACHENAR'S BEDROOM

Just to be safe, I went back to the generator, gave it numerous cranks, fired up ten more minutes of power.

Then I headed down the other tunnel. No surprise — another watertight door unsealed another bedroom. This one full of most interesting gadgetry. A sepulchral-looking ribcage lamp lit the room. Was this Achenar's? If so, it all displayed a pretty sick sense of humor.

I found the blue page on the bed:

I didn't take it, though. Remember, only one page can be carried at a time. This one's easier to get to, so I'll come back for it later — if I can.

I looked around a bit more. Across the room, atop a chest of drawers, sat a hologram device. When I turned it on, a beautiful rose appeared. Nice. But when I slid the lever across the bottom, the rose slowly mutated into a hideous skull.

Makes me wonder about a mind that can display such a thing. Is Achenar disturbed?

I looked in the drawers beneath. Nothing until I got to the second drawer from the bottom. There I found a journal page torn in half. Here's a couple shots of it:

Where's the other half? I'll definitely keep an eye out for it as I progress through these ages.

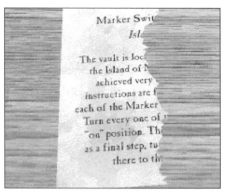

THE COMPASS ROOM

On a landing about halfway back up stairs, I noticed a red square insignia on the left wall. I was just about to explore it when the lights went out! Had to fumble my way up the dark stairs. I hurried out to the generator in the lighthouse, cranked it, hurried back.

When I touched the red square, a door opened. I entered, moved down a long crawlspace. At the end, a fabulous secret compass room. I stared at the windows. It was like an aquarium. Marine life wafted and drifted on the other side. This sealed compartment was completely underwater.

The compass itself was a thing of beauty. Buttons lined its perimeter, and I considered just punching random numbers. But then I remembered the blinking light in the telescope, set at — what was it?

I pulled out my journal, double-checked. Yes, set at 135 degrees.

I tried to click the corresponding compass button. But I hit the wrong one. Automatic power shutdown. Embarrassing. Had to fumble back upstairs again, crank up generator in the lighthouse again, then return. I finally set the compass correctly, pushing the 12th button clockwise from the north, at the tip of the lower right red triangle.

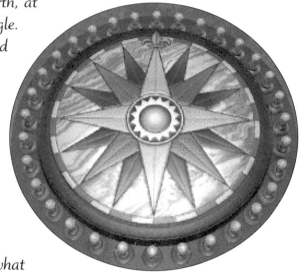

Suddenly the room was flooded with light. The source: A submersible lamp just beyond the window. The flashing light I saw in the telescope marks its position, no doubt. Then I remembered sketches of this lamp in the Stoneship journal back in the Myst library.

Ingenious. I know I keep repeating that word. But really, what else can I say?

THE STONESHIP BOOK ROOM

It seemed like time to try the final pump switch.

I went back to umbrella crow's nest, flipped the left switch, returned to boat. The stern cabin was now clear of water below deck. I went down an ornate stairway to the bookroom — like the compass room, it was lit by the submersible lamp on the other side of watertight windows.

As I approached the table in the center, the Myst book "morphed" up from the surface. I used it for a quick return to the Myst library.

RED PAGE #3

I slipped the red page into Sirrus's book. I could see and hear him better,
though the "transmission" (or whatever it was) still faded in and out through
static.

He spoke of being "freed from prison on this forgotten island of Myst." His warnings about his "wicked brother" and the blue pages were getting more urgent. Called Achenar "a man of distorted mind and senses … he disgusts me … do not release Achenar, his thirst for destruction is [unintelligible]."

Sirrus then mentioned two remaining red pages — then promised that if I help him I would be "greatly rewarded."

I had to sit and think about this awhile. Sirrus. Who is this guy? Clearly cooler, more rational than his brother. But something too slick about him. Too rehearsed.

And frankly, his solicitation gives me the creeps.

BLUE PAGE #3

This mystery is getting unsettling.

I just can't buy Sirrus completely. I don't like Achenar — geez, who could? — but I thought I should balance the input on this decision as much as I could.

So I went back to the Stoneship for the blue page.

It turned out to be a bit more tedious than I thought. I had to crank up the generator once and then go reset the compass to 135 degrees before I could get the submersible light to illuminate the book room below the ship. But eventually I made it.

Achenar sounded worse than ever, claiming now that it was Sirrus himself who imprisoned him in the blue book. He said I should beware his brother's "pretty speech," said Sirrus is dangerous, a killer in fact. He accused Sirrus of tricking their father, then suddenly howled, "hideously murdered our father, he'll murder you!"

Then more of the usual: Don't bring Sirrus the red pages, and so on — "his greed is endless."

Interestingly, he ends with: "You must obey me!"

My first thought: Oh yeah? You're a book. What are you gonna do — throw footnotes at me?

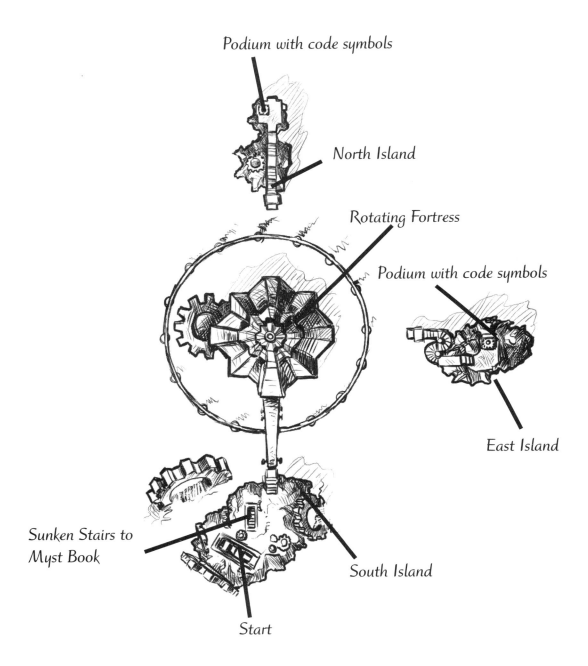

Podium with code symbols

North Island

Rotating Fortress

Podium with code symbols

East Island

Sunken Stairs to
Myst Book

South Island

Start

5. MECHANICAL AGE

THE CLOCK TOWER CODE

At the map, I reached out to the observatory icon again, this time holding on it until the beam settled red on the sunken gear icon at the lower-right.

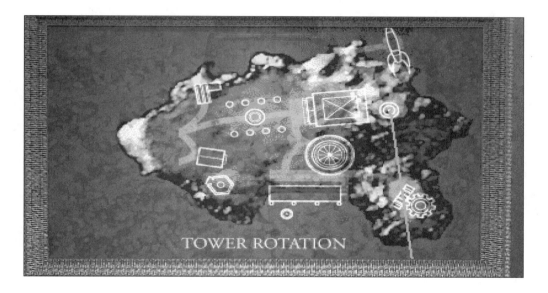

Back to the observatory. The tower had turned again. The lookout slot perfectly framed the sunken gear.

Up the "key" ladder. A plaque now centered at the top read:

Clock time of 2:40? Clock. Then it hit me. I left the library, went straight to the clock tower.

There, I turned the gear wheels to set the clock to 2:40. Then I pressed the red button ... and a truly remarkable bridge of gears rose from the water. I walked across to the clock tower door. Before entering, I flipped up the Marker Switch to the left. Think I've got all of them switched on now.

I entered the clock tower. Inside, I found a gear & lever device with three numbered wheels, stacked vertically. Now I understood the "2, 2, 1" part of the key message. The device was currently set at 3, 3, 3, and resetting it was tricky. Some experimenting revealed the following pattern:

PULL & RELEASE RIGHT LEVER - *moves the top two numbers one digit*

HOLD DOWN RIGHT LEVER - *moves top number one digit, but continues rotation of middle numbers*

PULL & RELEASE LEFT LEVER - *moves the bottom two numbers one digit*

HOLD DOWN LEFT LEVER - *moves bottom number one digit, but continues rotation of middle numbers*

I also learned that you can only change numbers until the counterweight on the left wall hits the ground. If that happens, you have to pull the lever on the back wall (right of the machine) to rewind and start over again at 3, 3, 3. Here's the best method I found to get 2, 2, 1:

Pull & release the right lever twice. This gets the 2 on top.

Hold the left lever down. This gets the 1 on bottom. Wait for the middle 2 to rotate back around. Listen for three clicks, then release immediately.

When I finally got the combination right, I heard mechanical grinding. Then, suddenly, the small gear on the contraption popped open, revealing a hidden compartment.

Nothing in it, but then I noticed its resemblance to the big gear on the platform by the dock. I remembered how the small replica ship in the basin modeled the behaviour of the sunken ship by the dock. This could be the same thing.

I hurried off to find out.

This was, of course, the case. And in the hidden compartment of the large raised gear was the book that would be my means of transportation to the Mechanical Age.

I opened the book and carefully observed the flyby of the island group. There was the fortress in the center, just as described in Atrus's journal, surrounded by the circular track I'd seen in his sketches. The three hills, now islands, lay to the south, north and east.

I made mental note of the layout as I touched the book and thus arrived at my destination.

THE MECHANICAL AGE

I returned to consciousness facing another huge, open gear. As I backed away from it, I could see that I was on the south island, connected by way of a bridge to the main fortress in the center.

Next to the gear was some kind of control panel with a four-symbol code access. I surmised that to return to Myst, I would have to discover the code somewhere on this metallic, circumscribed world. Next to the panel was a grooved sheet of metal, surrounded by railings. Probably the hidden stairway (now raised and locked) that I'd seen sketched in Atrus's Mechanical journal.

SIRRUS'S ROOM

I crossed the bridge to the fortress. Two hallways. I went left first, and ended up in Sirrus's room. Neat, gleaming, as usual. Refined taste. His gadgets and toys were pristine, clever, perfect. I stood at his chair, if you could call it that. More like the throne of a sun god.

I could just picture this kid.

Then I noticed a slightly recessed metal panel just to the right of the chair, near the floor, almost hidden by hanging tapestry. When I pushed it, it opened into a secret back room.

This place was a treasure trove. Full of gold, wines, and other treasures. I found the red page tucked amongst gold bars and coins in a chest at the back left corner of the room.

I also found a most interesting note from Achenar, scrolled and tucked in a slot on the right side of the wine rack.

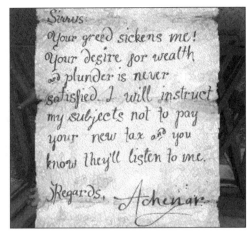

Sirrus—
Your greed sickens me!
Your desire for wealth
and plunder is never
satisfied. I will instruct
my subjects not to pay
your new tax and you
know they'll listen to me.

Regards, Achenar

ACHENAR'S ROOM

Achenar's room, as I'd come to expect, proved quite a contrast.

Weapons strewn about — maces, axes, crossed swords. A chilling death's head mask on the wall. But, most interesting (and actually useful) was the hologram "practice" device that Atrus had spoken of in his journal — a Fortress Rotation Simulator.

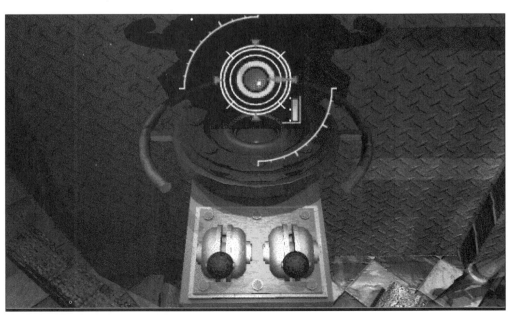

After calibrating itself, the simulator was ready. I played with it awhile. It seemed to have the same directional sound indicators as the Mazerunner in the Selenitic Age. Each sound let me know the simulated fortress was fully rotated to N, S, E, or W:

N	small clink
S	dull clank
W	bird chirp
E	air brake sound

Finally, I went back to exploring the room. Left of Achenar's blue throne, I found a recessed panel marked by a yellow line. Just like the one in Sirrus's room. I gave it a push and it easily opened into another secret room.

More grisly stuff. A butcher's cleaver on a bloodstained wooden cutting block. A desk that slid open to reveal a rotting skull. A shelf full of bottles and vials marked as poison.

Beneath the shelf, I found the blue page.

I left it for a return trip. Before leaving, I checked out the steel-bar cage in the room. I couldn't resist it — I had to flip the switch. I felt a tingle as a flash of electricity crackled through the bars! Wow. Gruesome. Giving me still more cause to wonder about the mental state of Achenar.

THE ELEVATOR

A back hallway, I discovered, connected the two rooms. Halfway down was a small corridor. At the head, a red button. At the far end, some sort of glassed-in compartment. My guess: An elevator.

But I could see no way to activate it, or even get in. I headed back to the red button, noticing the grooved floor. I had a hunch that this was another one of Atrus's trademark hidden staircases.

I pushed the red button. Bingo. The floor dropped into stairs, leading to a control room.

I took the control lever. A gentle push, and the central hub began to rotate. When it stopped, it clicked — and I noticed that the indicator at the left of the lever had changed. A couple more quick pushes and I'd lined up the openings in the pair of concentric circles on the indicator.

As they aligned, they turned red.

Obviously, I'd activated something.

I went back upstairs, pushed the red button to re-raise the floor. Then I headed down the corridor to the compartment. It was now open. Indeed, an elevator. I entered and pressed the down-arrow button. Buzzzz! Nothing. Then I pressed the middle button. The elevator went halfway up between floors — then stopped. So I pressed the up-arrow button.

Up I went. At the top, I hopped out, looked around. Nothing but the elevator.

I got back in and pushed the middle button again. This time it beeped six times (a timer, I wondered?), then the elevator dropped down halfway between floors and stopped again. Interesting. I pushed the up-arrow button again. When the elevator doors opened I pushed the middle button, hurried out and turned around.

The elevator dropped halfway, revealing a control panel exactly like the hologram device I'd played with in Achenar's room. This obviously was the real thing, however. It's the mechanism that rotates this fortress, linking the entry ramp with the three other islands around the perimeter.

It took a lot of trying and finessing, but I finally got the fortress facing the north island. I pressed the red button, stepped back as the elevator rose, then rode it down.

The footbridge now connected to the forbidding concrete slab of the north island. The only thing there was a metal plate atop a pedestal made of gears. On the plate, two icons. I recognized them from the control panel on the south island. Their position to the left of the plate led me to assume these were the first two icons of the exit code.

I returned to the fortress rotation controls to connect the bridge to the east island next. A side note: On the way back to the elevator, I passed through Sirrus's room again. Since the view was different, I took a peek through his spyglass again.

Here's what I saw:

Whose skeleton is hanging from the mast?

And equally to the point: Why does Sirrus have it fixed in his spyglass?

Anyway, as I said, I headed back up to the control room and got the fortress rotated to the east island. Then I went back out, and found an island much like the first I'd explored.

Another pedestal showed me the second pair of icons that I needed.

I had the code, but I needed to enter it in the control panel on the south island. So, back up to the control room.

I got the fortress rotated back south again, and hurried out.

When I got to the control panel, I entered the code sequence.

The metal platform (as I'd guessed) dropped into a stairway, revealing a passage to an underground room.

I went down ... and there sat the Myst book.

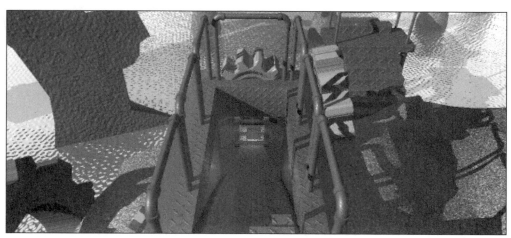

RED PAGE #4

Sirrus was most pleased with me. Gee, I can't tell you how that made me feel.

He said, "With each page I can see more clearly ... soon I will be free of this horrid prison, this book." He explained that there was only one remaining age to explore. Then he got to work on Achenar again. Said, "My brother is demented, he is guilty ... took advantage of the freedom father had given us ... do not retrieve the blue pages, he will destroy both myself and you as he destroyed other pages of Myst!"

Sirrus asserted that if I set Achenar free I would never escape him. "You will see that I am innocent and he is guilty." Then, as before, he offered me great rewards for coming down on his side and setting him free.

I still don't trust this guy.

BLUE PAGE #4

My return trip to Mechanical Age was swift, since no fortress rotation was necessary to pick up Achenar's blue page. When I returned with it, Achenar seemed more whacked-out than ever. At one point he pleaded, "Sirrus is guilty, do not release him ... he will destroy me, just as he destroyed —" Static, unfortunately, cut off the last word.

Achenar claims he was "an innocent bystander" and assumes that I've already observed Sirrus's unbridled lust for riches. He says Sirrus tricked others into believing that Achenar murdered his father! Now he's condemned to imprisonment in the book.

His final, pathetic howl — "I cannot bear it here for eternity!" — seemed genuine enough. But I can't say I'm even remotely convinced that his story is true.

Now, there should be only one age left to explore. Channelwood will be my next destination.

6. CHANNELWOOD AGE

THE TREE ELEVATOR

Back in the library, I thought about the Channelwood Age as described in Atrus's journal. A place of great forests and tree-dwellers. I went over to the island map. By now it was pretty clear — four ages, four "keys" to reaching them. During tower rotation, only four Marker Switch locations on the map prompted the holographic beam to turn red. The three I'd tried so far had revealed a "key" plaque in the tower. Only one remained.

I rotated the tower until the beam turned red over the Marker Switch location at the log cabin. But I looked closer. I hadn't noticed before — it was not precisely on the cabin itself. An icon for something behind the cabin activated the red beam.

I remembered the giant tree, the platform. But how did it work?

I hurried up to the tower, climbed to the viewing slot. The slot indeed framed the tree:

Interesting. But the cabin had to be part of the puzzle too, it seemed. I went to the "key" ladder, anxious to see what clue it might provide. Here's the plaque I saw at the top:

Next, I went to the tree. A close exploration revealed nothing but a tree, a platform — no buttons, no code mechanisms. Nothing. I went in the cabin, stared at the furnace, the pressure compartment. The pilot flame box. The gauge. Nothing again.

I turned to go.

And there it was. The safe! Of course. A three-number combination, staring me in the face. I quickly entered the key code numbers on the combination lock.

Inside — a book of matches!

I opened the matchbox, took a match, then struck it on the box flint. It lept to flame. Then I turned to the bottom left of the furnace and lit the pilot light — a small yellow spot on the square opening there. Finally, I pulled on the right side of the wheel, and gave it 10 or 12 good clockwise cranks until it wouldn't turn anymore.

That got the flame burning brightly.

Immediately, I heard odd booming sounds as the gauge showed the pressure build up. The loud sounds seemed to be coming from out back. I rushed out to the giant tree. Everything seemed the same, until I looked up. About 100 feet off the ground was a door carved into the trunk — a tree elevator! But now, how to get it back down?

Obviously, I had to turn off the gas.

I went back into the cabin and did just that, yanking counterclockwise until the fire died. Immediately, more booming sounds. I strolled out to the base of the tree, but as I approached I saw the door drop into the ground. I missed it!

So I had to repeat the process. But this time I hurried out at the very instant the furnace flame died, then headed straight for the tree platform. I waited until the open door dropped to ground level.

I hopped in the elevator door just in the nick of time and rode down to an underground room. There, I found the Channelwood passage book lying on a stump. I opened it, and was on my way.

CHANNELWOOD AGE

I found myself on an amazing series of wooden walkways suspended above water. Trees everywhere, rising from the water. As I began to explore, I noticed a system of interconnected pipes running along most of the walkways. Listening, I could hear nothing flowing through them. A quick look around made it obvious to me that a map would be necessary, so I'll start one here.

Channelwood Lower Level Walkways

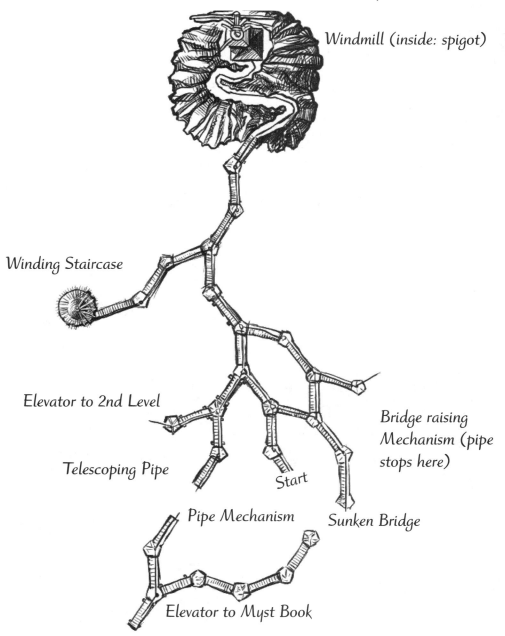

Windmill (inside: spigot)

Winding Staircase

Elevator to 2nd Level

Bridge raising
Mechanism (pipe
stops here)

Telescoping Pipe

Start

Sunken Bridge

Pipe Mechanism

Elevator to Myst Book

In the distance I saw a twirling windmill. I worked my way to it pretty easily — all the pipes and pathways seemed to lead there.

I entered the structure. Explored. Saw that it was pumping water up from the surrounding body of water into a large tank. I noticed a spigot down at the base of the tank. I figured that opening it would let water flow through the pipe system below.

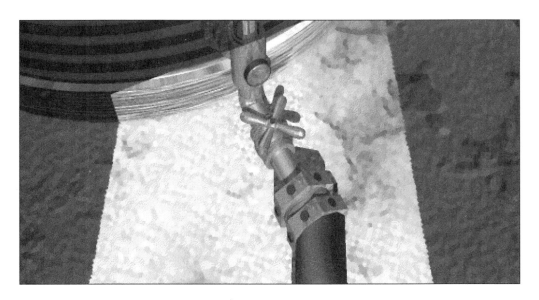

I twisted the spigot counterclockwise. Water gurgled down the pipes behind me.

I followed the path back down. But now I could hear water bubbling all the way to the first fork in the walkway. There, I examined what looked like a switching device: Yellow dots in a Y split, with a metal switch I could flip back and forth to cover one branch of the Y or the other.

When I walked down the left fork, in the direction of the uncovered yellow dots, I could hear the water in the pipes. But when I went down the other fork, the one blocked by the switch, I could hear no water in the pipes. I flipped the lever on the device. Now the opposite was true. Yes, it's a routing switch.

Up ahead to the right, I saw a winding staircase. I routed the water to the right, down that path. As I approached, I noticed that the water pipe ended at some kind of hydraulic mechanism.

And it hit me — this piping system doesn't just provide running water in Channelwood. It's a power source!

Everything here runs on water power.

Unfortunately, power or no, I could find no way to open the door at the bottom of the staircase. Apparently it can only be opened from the inside.

I headed back to the first fork, then sat down to update the journal. That's where I am now as I write these words. From here, I can see some kind of crude rope-operated elevator ahead.

Looking up, I can see an intercon nected system of huts in the treetops.

My next goal: I want to get up into that second level.

Well, I got my wish. I'm sitting in a treehouse.

I feel like a kid again. Lookin' around, kickin' my feet. Too bad I've got the treachery and betrayal of a dysfunctional family to deal with.

I could almost enjoy this place.

Here's how I got here.

Back at the first fork I rerouted water down the left fork. Then I worked my way to the elevator, routing the water right three more times until it piped into the elevator mechanism.

I got in, closed the door, pulled the handle and rode to the second level.

I stepped out into an amazing but deteriorating treehouse complex. One glance around reminded me of the sketch in the Channelwood journal. I retrieved it from my photo pouch.

A little exploration showed me that this indeed was a map of this second level. Here it is:

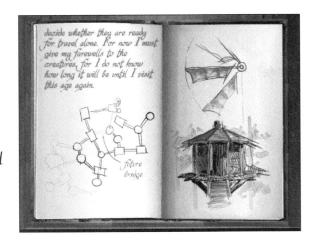

I have to admit that I did a lot of wandering around. I eventually worked my way over to the winding staircase. Fairly easy, using the map. Next to it, an elevator to a third level! I was momentarily excited.

But then I remembered: I had to direct water away from this elevator's power mechanism at the bottom of the winding staircase in order to get power to the other elevator. Can't power both at the same time! Big problem. If I could use the winding stairs, then I wouldn't need the other elevator. But of course here's big problem #2.

The door leading down to the ground is locked.

Good news!

I examined the map again. Noticed a dotted line running from the winding staircase to one of the huts. On a hunch, I went to that hut and found a small red switch.

I went to it, noticing that the view looked across at the winding staircase. When I threw the switch, the second-level staircase door opened! Using the map, I worked my way over to the stairs, went down, and threw open the lower-level door from the inside. Then I walked out to the first fork in the pipes and switched the water flow toward the staircase.

I believe I'm now ready to take the third level.

This brother situation gets creepier by the minute.

The third level, it turns out, contains the rooms of Sirrus and Achenar. Here's what I found.

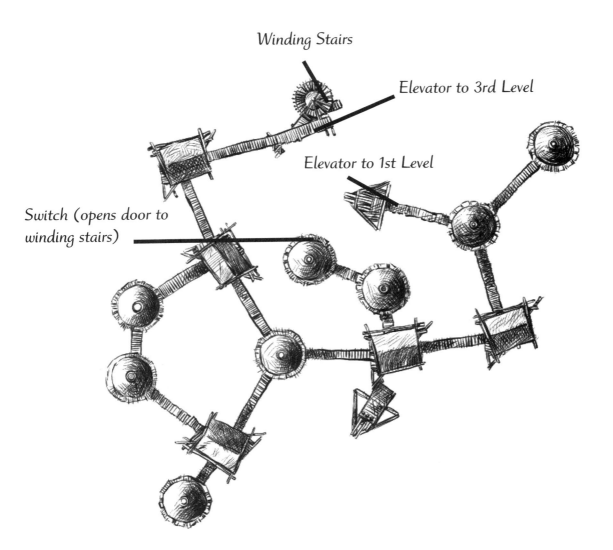

Winding Stairs

Elevator to 3rd Level

Elevator to 1st Level

Switch (opens door to
winding stairs)

The Channelwood Age

Achenar's Bedroom

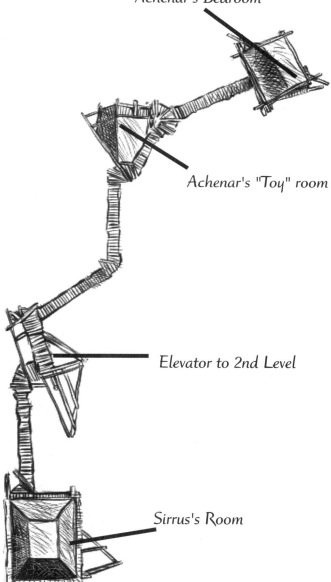

Achenar's "Toy" room

Elevator to 2nd Level

Sirrus's Room

ACHENAR'S ROOMS

The first thing I came to was an eery, paint-splattered hut with a metallic door. The door swung open easily, I stepped inside ... and got the fright of my life. Suddenly, an image of Achenar appeared in midair. Saying something ugly and menacing. Guttural foreign tongue.

I remembered that, in the Channelwood Age book, Atrus mentioned how his sons had learned the tree-dweller's language quickly. OK, fine. But this room, man. Downright demonic decorating. Ritualistic candles, eerie masks. And more of those eccentric and even dangerous toys. Dark and disturbed mind here. I'm truly beginning to wonder about Achenar and the blue pages — do I dare free this sick loon?

I followed the footbridge further to Achenar's bedroom, where I found the last blue page.

It sat next to another hologram device with four buttons. The first two from the left triggered more odd, menacing messages from Achenar. The third brought up the same message I'd seen when entering his room. But the button on the right gave me another surprise — Sirrus!

His image said: "I hope I pushed the right button. Very interesting device, brother. I'm not erasing anything important, am I? (evil laugh) He is ... preparing. Remember, take only one page."

What the hell does that mean?

These guys truly belong in a book.

On the way back toward the elevator, I peeked back in the first room. Sure enough, the hologram triggered there now was that of Sirrus.

SIRRUS'S ROOM

As I returned to the elevator, I noticed a walkway branching around it to the right. I followed it to Sirrus's bedroom. As usual, the place was first class, except for a few empty wine bottles strewn about.

I found the final red page in the desk drawer on the left, the one beneath the window view of the windmill.

I found some other interesting artifacts, too.

The bed rested on a pedestal which contained two drawers under the bed. In the left drawer I found a deadly-looking dagger. In the other drawer, more empty wine bottles — I thought of the drugs I'd found back on the Stoneship. And underneath them was the other half of the torn journal page I'd found in Achenar's Stoneship bedroom.

I pulled out the other one, then put them together to get this message:

Marker Switch Vault Access
Island of Myst

The vault is located in very plain view on the Island of Myst, and access can be achieved very easily if these simple instructions are followed. First, locate each of the Marker Switches on the island. Turn every one of these switches to the "on" position. Then go to the dock and, as a final step, turn the Marker Switch there to the "off" position.

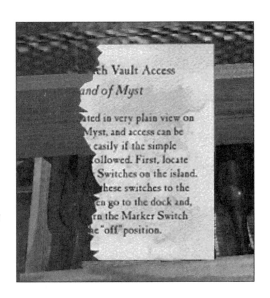

Now it's decision time. Which page, red or blue, goes back to Myst?

Neither one seems right. So I'll do what any thinking man would do —
flip a coin.

Tails. Achenar wins.

I left the red page where it was.

Getting back, however, is proving somewhat tricky.

I knew there must be a return book somewhere. I figure the far elevator
— the one I'd seen at the far end of Channelwood — has to be my passage
to the Myst book.

But directing water power to it has required some work.

THE HIDDEN BRIDGE

OK. It took hours of trial, error, and mapping. But here's what I eventually
came up with:

First, I went down the winding staircase and out to the first fork. There I
directed the water left. I did the same at the next switch. The next left fork,
however, led to a dead end, so I directed water right.

The next fork had no switch, so I went left, coming to what seemed like
another dead end. But I pulled the handle on a mechanism there. A hidden
bridge rose from the water. Very Atrus design.

I took this shot as it was happening:

Unfortunately, the water pipes end here. Now what?

THE TELESCOPING PIPE

Success! It took some doing, but it got done.

Here's how:

From the hidden bridge, I kept going to the far elevator. Its water pipes came in from a different direction. I followed the pipes until they ended at a disconnected section of pipe. For a moment, I felt panic. Was I stranded here? The sound of bird chirps was already driving me crazy. A lifetime here would turn me into — I don't know, maybe Achenar.

But then I noticed a crank on the pipe below me.

I turned it. A section of pipe began to telescope across the gap, connecting to the pipe on the other side.

I was so excited, I snapped a shot of this in progress:

The key now was to direct water power across this section of pipe to the far elevator, then hopefully punch my ticket to Myst. I went back to the first

Y fork, consulted my map, then redirected the water in this order — left, right, right, then left.

This sent the water down across the telescoped pipe. I used my map again to get around to the far elevator, rode it up ... and there, indeed, was the Myst book waiting for me at the top.

BLUE PAGE #5

I put the last blue page in Achenar's book and braced myself for the worst.

He appeared on the page, but did not leap at my throat from the book as I half-expected. Instead I learned that there was still another page, hidden in a secret compartment that I could reach through the Library fireplace. Of course, he spat some more invective against Sirrus. True brotherly love. Wow. Keep these guys away from Philadelphia.

Finally, he told me about the Pattern Book on the middle shelf of the library, which I'd already discovered. It contains a pattern — number 158, he said — that I can enter on the door of the fireplace. This will get me to the secret chamber.

Not ready to fully trust such a certified candidate for institutionalization, I've decided to do as I've done in the other ages — return to Channelwood for the other brother's page.

I like to experience the full spectrum of hatred before I make these kinds of decisions.

Well, I'm back. It was indeed quick. By now I've gotten pretty adept at moving around in the odd logic of this world. So, yes, the task was completed with a certain alacrity.

(Geez, I'm beginning to write like these guys talk.)

A side note, though: On the way back to Channelwood, the adolescent in me had to play in the redwood elevator just a bit.

I'd noticed another pressure valve wheel down in the book room. I twisted it clockwise, and quickly hopped in the door.

Soon I was a hundred feet high, enjoying the panoramic view. Here's a shot of what I saw:

To get back down, I held in the button by the door. Loud hiss, steam releasing. Unfortunately, this control only got me to ground level. I had to hop back in the cabin, turn the pressure wheel down, then hurry back out and hop in the elevator again.

Back down to the book room.
Then off to Channelwood.

RED PAGE #5

This time, I needed only one water pipe switch. On arrival, I went to the first valve and directed water right, toward the winding stairs. Then up for the red page, back down the elevator and stairs, and back to the first valve, where I redirected the water to the left again. Then a quick jaunt to the far elevator, and up to the book room.

Back to Myst library. And another scintillating exchange with Sirrus.

OK, Sirrus is clearly saner in a literal sense — doesn't drool, giggle like an idiot, and so on. But I don't know. I read somewhere that we share the same basic brainstem with lizards. Listening to this guy trips some little lizard alarm in me: Danger! Danger! His melodramatic "debt of gratitude" gives me a chill, and his overbaked protestations of innocence are starting to annoy me.

Like Achenar, he gave me the back story — his version, of course. He ripped his brother for a while, then directed me to pattern 158 and the fireplace. He, too, warned me not to touch either the green book or the blue page. Very interesting.

Before trying the secret fireplace chamber, however, I wanted to check out the Marker Switch Vault Access mentioned in the now-combined halves of the torn journal page.

ENDGAME

MARKER SWITCH VAULT

As far as I knew, I'd turned on all of the Marker Switches on the Island of Myst. So I headed straight for the dock switch and flipped it off. A front compartment swung open.

Inside, a white page!

Now what? I scoured my journal, looking for any mention of a white page. Nothing. What does this mean?

I took the page and returned to the library.

THE FIREPLACE PASSAGE

So I'm sitting here in a brick chamber, ruminating on the decision of my life.

Some fresh air would be nice. OK, the fireplace is spotless, like everything else in Myst. But I'm choking on the dust of this decision — because frankly, I don't trust either of these guys. I don't buy their stories, don't like their attitudes. Don't like their facial hair.

But I'm jumping ahead. Let me quickly describe how I got here:

First, I went to the bookshelf (as instructed) and pulled out the Pattern Book. I flipped to page 158 and snapped a photo. Then I went in the fireplace, pushed the red button, and entered the pattern code on the door:

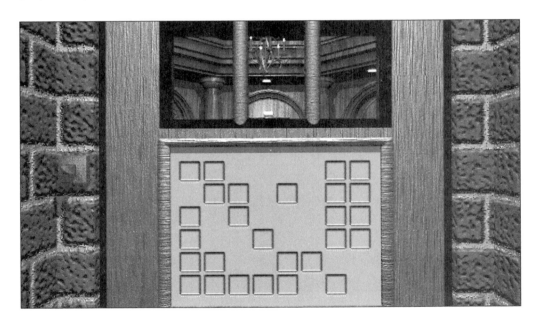

I pushed the button again. Gears engaged, mechanisms kicked in. Another Myst moment. I was transported to a secret chamber, just as both brothers had described. There, indeed, sat the last red and blue pages. Also the dreaded Green Book, about which both brothers had fervently warned me. So this is it.

All of it coming down to a simple question:
Who do you trust?

My answer: Nobody.

OK, so maybe it's not so great to be cynical by nature. But in this case it paid off big time.

That's right. Red or blue? I chose neither.

I followed an instinct which told me that if these two guys, Sirrus and Achenar, are telling me, <u>Don't touch the Green Book!</u> — then that's exactly what I should do. I opened it.

And there, on the living page, sat none other than Atrus himself!

He told me he is in a place called Dunny. Then he told his story. He spoke of the books he writes, books that link him to fantastic places. Says it's "an art I learned from my father many years ago." He mentioned the red and blue books, actually written as traps for greedy explorers. Which led him to his boys, their abuse of privilege, their dreams of riches and power. He seemed genuinely sad at the betrayal.

I decided I could actually like this man.

Finally, he spoke of being trapped himself, in Dunny. A single page from his Myst linking book was missing. He could not travel back to his home island without it.

I correctly assumed he meant the white page I had with me. I placed my hand on the illustration in the Green Book ... and was transported to Dunny, where I now stood face to face with Atrus.

I gave him the white page. He placed it in his Myst linking book. Then he considered his sons, and what he must do. He placed his hand on the book, saying he'd be back shortly.

When he returned, he worried about the time lost from his writing, worried that his delay may have already had a "catastrophic effect" on the world where his wife Catherine is being held hostage. He offered me the Myst library as a show of gratitude ... then concluded with these chilling words: "I am fighting a foe much greater than my sons could even imagine." At some point in the future, he said, he may need my assistance again.

I nodded.

Finally, he handed me the Myst book to return to the Myst library. I did so. And when I got there, I found charred blast marks where the red and blue books had once sat on display.

Myst

Quick Guide

QUICK GUIDE TO MYST ISLAND

Here's a quick walkthrough of all the steps you'll need to take to unlock the secrets of Myst. Keep in mind that the game does not have a strictly linear structure. You can explore the four Ages — Selenitic, Stoneship, Mechanical and Channelwood — in any order you wish. Our solution sequence was chosen arbitrarily.

We'll start with an explanation of the Map mechanism in the Library. Understanding how the Map works is the key to unlocking the other wonders of Myst, including travel to the four Ages.

Important: Please read the following section about the Map first! Much of the Walkthrough is based on the assumption that you know how the Map works.

About the Map in the Library

Each time you activate a Marker Switch (i.e., flip up its handle) on the Island, a corresponding icon is activated on the Map in the Myst Library. When you approach the Map, these activated icons light up. You can then use the Map to rotate the observation tower to view the island landmarks represented by each icon. This rotation reveals important clues inside the tower.

Here's how the Map works:

1) First, activate the Marker Switches at these four locations on the island: dock, sunken gear, spaceship, and log cabin. (You need to turn on all eight Marker Switches to complete Myst, but these four are

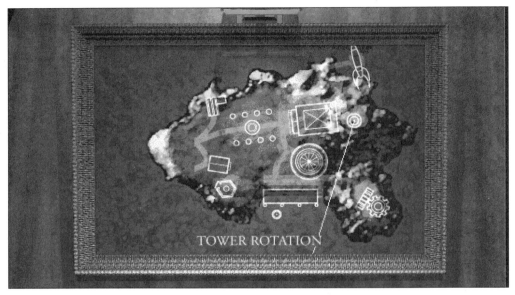

TOWER ROTATION

the only ones necessary for transportation to other Ages.)

2) Go to the Map. Click & hold on the tower icon (flashing concentric circles) at the Map's far right. This activates a white beam which swings in an arc around the Map.

3) Notice that the beam turns red when it passes over the four icons that correspond to the four locations mentioned previously. Release the mouse button when the beam turns red — for example, over the spaceship icon. You'll hear the tower rotate until the viewing slot faces the location represented by the icon on the Map — in this case, the spaceship on its launch pad.

4) Now approach the bookshelf painting (to the left of the bookshelf) and click on it. When the secret passageway appears behind the bookshelf, follow it to the elevator.

5) Click on the elevator door to close it, then click on the blue button that reads "Library." This takes you up to the tower. Click on the door again to open it.

6) If you want, you can climb the ladder directly in front of you.

The Elevator

The First Ladder

You'll see that the viewing slot now frames the location you designated on the Map. (Again, in this example, the spaceship.)

7) Go around behind the elevator and climb the "key" ladder (i.e., the ladder marked with the key inscription). At the top, you'll find a plaque inscribed with a clue.

Now you need to figure out what the clue means, where and how it can be implemented, and so on. For more on each of the four clues you'll find in the tower,

The Key Ladder

read the rest of this walkthrough.

The Object of Myst

Overall, your goal is to uncover the story of Adrus and his sons, Sirrus and Achenar, then decide who is telling the truth, who is lying, who should be set free.

More specifically, you need to:

1) Bring the red and/or blue pages from each Age back to the Library, place them in their respective books, and view messages from Sirrus and Achenar. Ultimately, you must choose freedom or continued imprisonment for each brother.

2) Find and combine the two halves of a torn journal page in order to gain access to the Marker Switch Vault on Myst Island.

3) Discover the access code to a secret compartment in the Library, where you will make your final decisions.

About Red and Blue Pages

Each Age holds one red page and one blue page. One of your primary goals, as mentioned above, is to bring them back. But note: Only one page can be carried at a time. If you're already holding the red page and try to pick up the blue page, the red page will automatically transport back to where you found it.

So in order to get both pages, you'll have to bring one back to Myst Island, then make a return trip to the Age to get the other one. This isn't particularly difficult, however. Once you've solved a puzzle in Myst, it stays solved. For example, if you've entered a code into a portal mechanism, it will still be entered upon your return.

You don't need to bring both pages back from every Age in order to complete the game. If you decide after the first viewing that you want to help only Sirrus and not Achenar, you can bring back only the red page from each Age. Or vice-versa. But in order to get the final clue, you'll need to bring all of the red pages OR all of the blue pages. You can't just bring two red pages and two blue pages, for example.

About the Dimensional Imager

In the forechamber behind the recessed door in the dock, you'll discover a device called a Dimensional Imager. You don't need to find the Imager to complete the game, but it's kind of fun to play with. The control panel is on the wall by the exit. Click on the button at the upper left to open the front cover. You can enter each of the three codes listed on the cover of the panel (40, 47, 67) and view those images by pressing the button on the front of the Imager itself.

 If you read the note that Adrus left for Catherine on the lawn by the Planetarium (hard to miss), you know that you can view an

additional 3-D image if you enter the number of Marker Switches on the island into the control panel. You can wander around the island counting the switches, or you can read the next few words in which we tell you that the correct number is "8."

 Enter "08" into the Imager and meet Adrus.

MYST ISLAND LOCATIONS

The first thing you should do upon arriving in Myst is explore, turning on Marker

Switches wherever you find them. Here's a quick list of the important locations on the island. Locations with Marker Switches are noted:

The Dock

Marker Switch here. No exploration necessary. This is where you

The Dock Marker Switch

begin the game. Note the sunken ship to the right and the door recessed into the retaining wall to the left.

The Dock Forechamber

This chamber lies behind the recessed door at the dock. It contains the Dimensional Imager.

The Sunken Gear

Marker Switch here. Straight ahead up the steps from the dock.

The Dock Forechamber Entry

The Planetarium

The Sunken Gear

Marker Switch here. Up the stairs from the dock, first building on the right.

The Library

Up stairs from the dock, second building on the right.

The Planetarium

The Observation Tower

The Library

Sits on the peak behind the Library. You can only get to it via an elevator found at the end of a secret passageway in the Library.

The Spaceship

Marker Switch here. Down a ramp on a platform to the left of the Library. Note the Breaker Tower (with breaker switch at the top of its ladder) to the left of the ramp.

The Pillar Garden

Marker Switch here. This is the path leading straight away from the

The Spaceship

entrance of the Library. Objects of interest — the basin with the ship

The Pillar Garden & Ship

model, and the inscribed markers at the base of each pillar.

The Generator Cave

Marker Switch here. This is the brick structure further down the path, just past the Pillar Garden. Downstairs is the generator room. Note the Breaker Tower (with breaker switch at the top of its ladder) just to the right of the structure.

The Generator

The Log Cabin

Marker Switch here. The cabin is hidden in trees down the left side the path, not far from the Generator building.

The Giant Tree Platform

Behind the Log Cabin, to the right.

The Cabin

The Clocktower

Marker Switch here (though you can't actually reach it until you find the clocktower access code.) Sits offshore at the end of the path leading away from the Library. Note the control mechanism on the shore.

GETTING

The Clocktower

The Tree Elevator

Myst Island

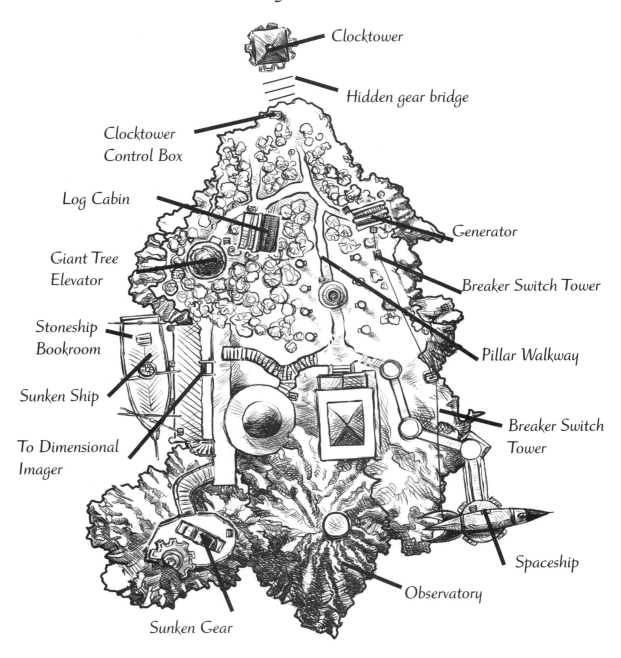

Clocktower

Hidden gear bridge

Clocktower
Control Box

Log Cabin

Generator

Giant Tree
Elevator

Breaker Switch Tower

Stoneship
Bookroom

Pillar Walkway

Sunken Ship

Breaker Switch
Tower

To Dimensional
Imager

Spaceship

Observatory

Sunken Gear

FROM MYST ISLAND
TO THE SELENITIC AGE:

1) Activate the Marker Switch next to the the Spaceship (if you haven't already), then return to the Library.

2) In the Library, go to the bookshelf. Click on the blue book that sits tilted on the middle shelf, then turn to the page with the keyboard sequence. Copy down the sequence.

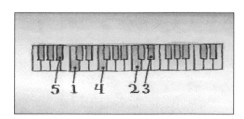

3) Now go to the Map. Click & hold on the tower icon until the beam rotates and "locks on" (turns red) over the Spaceship icon.

4) Go to the observatory tower. (If you don't know how yet, refer back to About the Map in the Library.) The lookout slot should be lined up to view the Spaceship.

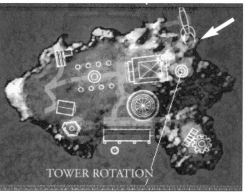

TOWER ROTATION

5) Go behind the elevator and climb the ladder with the "key" insignia. The plaque at the top should read "59 volts."

6) Go to the generator cave. There are ten generators. Each can be turned on/off by clicking on one of the buttons (two rows of five) on the control panel.

Note: Each generator has a different voltage. You need to activate a combination of generators whose voltage adds up to 59 volts in order to power up the Spaceship.

7) If you select a combination that adds up to more than 59 volts, you trip a breaker switch which cuts power to the Spaceship (measured on the control panel's right gauge) to zero. If this happens, you'll have to go out and check the Breaker Towers and see which of the two switches was tripped. (The tripped switch will be in the down position.) Just click on the tripped switch to throw it back up.

8) Of course, you can avoid tripped switches by simply pressing these generator buttons:

LEFT ROW	**RIGHT ROW**
one (10v)	**three (22v)**
three (18v)	**four (19v)**

9) Go to the Spaceship. When you click on the door, it will open. Enter and go to the keyboard to the right. Play the five-note keyboard sequence you copied from the Selenitic journal in the library, and listen carefully.

10) Go to the tuner at the other end of the Spaceship and enter the sequence in order from left to right by moving the slider bars.

Note: If you don't have great aural retention, you may have to play the first note on the keyboard, then go enter it on the tuner, return and play the second note, go back to tuner and enter it, and so on, until all five notes are entered in sequence.

11) Pull the handle on the tuner mechanism. The "transport" book will appear in the viewscreen.

The Selenitic Age

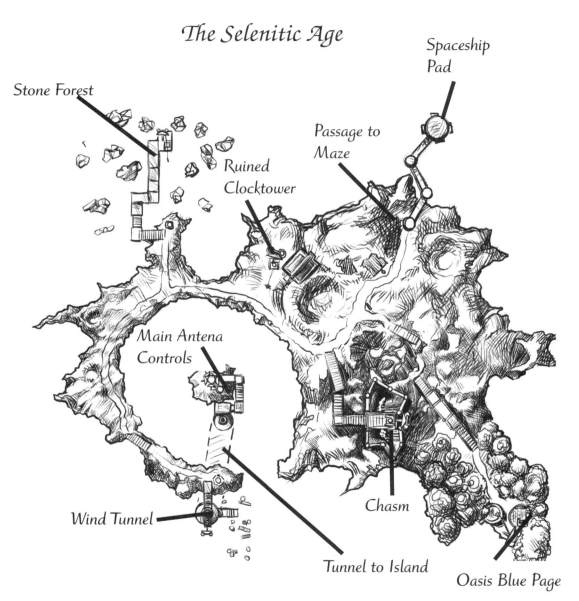

Spaceship Pad

Stone Forest

Passage to Maze

Ruined Clocktower

Main Antena Controls

Wind Tunnel

Chasm

Tunnel to Island

Oasis Blue Page

12) Click on the book to see an animated "flyby" of the Selenitic Age island.

13) Click on the viewscreen again to be transported to the Selenitic Age.

SELENITIC AGE

The main puzzle here is to discover a five-sound sequence that you can enter into the slider-bar mechanism at the portal door. (The portal is the first structure you encounter after leaving the Spaceship.) Once you enter the correct code, you can open the door and go down to the Mazerunner. Here's what to do:

1) Travel around the Age and turn on each transmitter. There are five in all. Each one is activated in the same way: Simply click on the red button beneath the golden icon on each podium. This switches on a nearby microphone, which picks up that location's sound and transmits it to a central receiver on the island in the middle of the lagoon.

Tip: Each of the icons on the antenna podiums is associated with the particular sound at that location. It's a good idea to sketch all the icons and describe each associated sound.

2) Remember to pick up a red or blue page when you find it. But also remember: You can only bring back one page at a time. To get both, you'll have to make a return trip.

3) There are five transmitter locations in all:

a) The Chasm. Just past the portal is a brick stairway to the left of the path. Follow this up to a platform over the chasm.

b) The Oasis. From the bottom of the chasm stairs, look back in the direction of the Spaceship. To the left is the portal structure. To the right, you'll see a worn path. Follow that path to a lush, green oasis. Also note: You'll find the Blue Page on a platform to the left of the main podium at the oasis.

  c) The Clocktower Ruins. From the portal, follow the path past the chasm stairway. The clocktower will loom ahead on your right.

  d) The Stone Forest. Proceed past the clocktower down the narrow peninsula to a Y-branch. Take the right fork out to an offshore platform. Note: The Red Page sits atop the podium here.

  e) The Windtunnel. Take the left fork at the Y-branch in the peninsula.

 4) The windtunnel podium sits behind an opening that looks like a well. After you've activated the microphone, go down the ladder and follow the tunnel to another ladder. (The switch at the bottom turns on a tunnel light, but you don't absolutely need it to traverse the tunnel.) Go up the far ladder.

 5) Click on the main antenna podium to open the steel doors.

 6) Five camera/receivers face O degrees from this main podium. Your task is to aim them at the five transmitters on the island, then press the Σ button to get the proper code sequence to enter in the portal door slider mechanism.

  If you want the simple solution, skip to #7. If you want to solve this puzzle step-by-step, here's what to do:

  a) Click on the first button (the Oasis icon), then click on the arrows to swing the camera around in a 360 degree arc. Move in small increments, then stop and listen for the sound that corresponds to the icon on the button — in this case, running water.

  b) When you get within 5 degrees of the correct alignment, the sound faintly appears and the appropriate directional arrow flashes, showing you which way to rotate the camera.

  c) When you hit the exact degree mark, the static disappears and the sound "locks in" clearly.

d) Repeat this process with the other four icon buttons.

e) When you've got all five receivers aligned, press the Σ button at the bottom. The portal code sound sequence will play, so jot it down in the correct order. Remember: The portal slider-bar mechanism relies on sound only. If you have poor sound memory, you might want to make a note describing each sound in the sequence.

7) Here, for the impatient, are the proper camera/receiver alignments and the code sequence:

1	Stone Forest	15.0
2	Oasis	153.4
3	Windtunnel	212.2
4	Chasm	130.3
5	Clock	55.6

8) Go back to the portal door and input the sounds from left to right in the order listed in #7. Push the button.

9) Go down the passageway to the Mazerunner rail car. Click on the blue button to open the door, get in the car, then sit in the driver's seat.

10) Click on FORWARD to lower the Mazerunner into the maze. Then navigate the maze by clicking on the arrow buttons to select directions according to the sound cues

given. (If you miss the cue, replay it by pressing the red button on the control panel.)

Here are the sound/direction cues:

N	small bell	bing
S	dull bell	clank
E	airbrake	fwssss
W	bird	twrrrreeee

NW, NE, SW, SE combine sounds of the two directions

Also note: The BACKTRACK button is "smart." When you click on it, the Mazerunner automatically moves back toward the last correct position on the track.

11) Here is the correct mazerunning sequence: N, W, N, E, E, S, S, W, SW, W, NW, NE, N, SE and out.

12) At the end of the maze, exit the Mazerunner. Go down the tunnel to the Myst book.

13) Click on the book to open it, then click on the picture of the library ceiling on the right-hand page. You will be returned to the Myst library.

14) OPTIONAL: After putting the page in the appropriate colored book and viewing the new message from the brother, you can return to the Selenitic Age for the other page. Simply go to the Spaceship again, click twice on the viewscreen (the correct code is still loaded), exit the ship, then retrieve the page. Go back to the portal door (again, the code is already loaded) and renegotiate the maze to return again to Myst.

GETTING FROM MYST ISLAND
TO THE STONESHIP AGE:

1) Activate the Marker Switch at the Myst dock (if you haven't already), then return to the Library.

2) Now go to the Map. Click & hold on the tower icon until the beam rotates and "locks on" (turns red) over the dock icon.

3) Go to the observatory tower. (If you don't know how yet, refer back to About the Map in the Library.) The lookout slot should be lined up to view the sunken ship.

4) Go behind the elevator and climb the ladder with the "key" insignia. The plaque at the top will display the following:

5) Go next to the Planetarium, sit in the chair, and pull down the star plotter.

6) Enter the first date & time into the plotter, then press the button at the upper left. A constellation appears.

7) Carefully sketch the constellation, then repeat the process for the other two star dates.

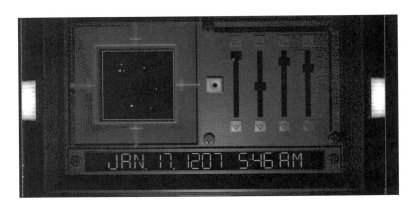

8) Go back to the Library bookshelf. Click on the blue & red book that sits on the far right of the top shelf, then turn to the pages with the constellation drawings. Match the Stoneship journal drawings to your sketches.

You should find: Leaf, Snake, Insect.

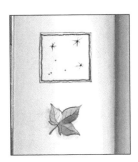
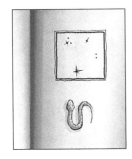

9) Go outside to the Pillar Garden and click on the Leaf, Snake and Insect markers. (Each insignia turns green when "on.") You'll hear a rushing of water as both the boat model in the basin and the actual boat by the dock rise up and float.

10) Go down to the dock, board the boat, and enter the aft cabin compartment. You'll find the Stoneship transport book.

11) Click on the book to open it and activate the flyby animation, then click on the picture to transport to the Stoneship Age.

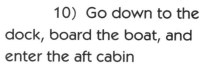

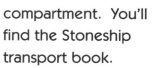

STONESHIP AGE

1) Go to the umbrella crow's nest. The three switches there pump out water in various parts of the ship/island:

RIGHT SWITCH	**Pumps out lighthouse**
MIDDLE SWITCH	**Pumps out stoneship tunnels**
LEFT SWITCH	**Pumps out hold in ship's aft (book room)**

The Stoneship Age

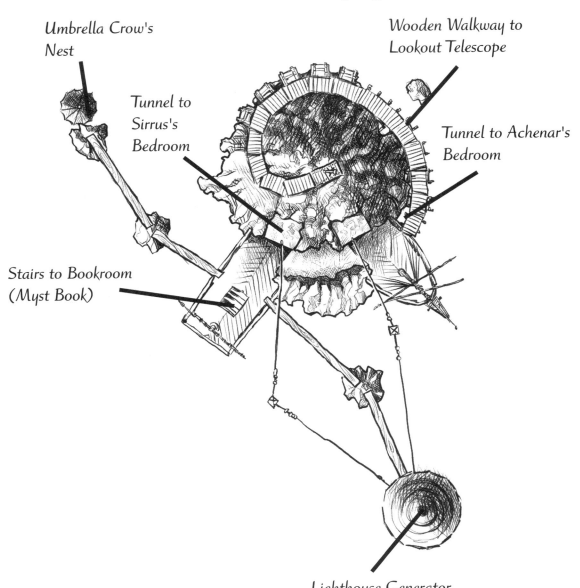

Umbrella Crow's Nest

Tunnel to Sirrus's Bedroom

Wooden Walkway to Lookout Telescope

Tunnel to Achenar's Bedroom

Stairs to Bookroom (Myst Book)

Lighthouse Generator

2) Click on the right switch to pump out the lighthouse. Now enter the lighthouse.

3) Go downstairs and click on the spigot at the bottom left of the trunk. When the water finishes draining from the trunk, click on the spigot again to shut it (making the trunk watertight).

4) Now go back to the crow's nest and click on the middle switch to pump out the ship's tunnels and re-flood the lighthouse.

5) Return to the lighthouse. The trunk is now floating next to the key chained to the floor. Click on the key to unlock the trunk. You'll find another key inside.

6) Take the key from inside the trunk. Climb the ladder and use the key to open the attic door.

7) Upstairs you'll find a generator with a battery pack. Click and hold on the generator to crank it up, which recharges the battery. Click on the battery to check the charge meter. The light will run to the top of the meter when it's fully charged, which gives you about ten minutes of power to explore the ship.

8) This next step is not essential, but it does give you a clue for a later puzzle. Go up the wooden bridge path to the lookout telescope. If you scan the horizon, you'll find a blinking light. (The light won't blink if you haven't fired up the generator yet.) Note the compass direction of 135 degrees.

The Lookout

9) Now go in the ship and explore the brothers' bedrooms. Sirrus bunked in the room down the stairs leading off the rear half of the ship, Achenar in the room off the front half. Remember: You can take only one page at a time.

10) In Sirrus's room, find the red page in the bottom drawer of his dresser chest.

11) In Achenar's room, find the blue page on the bed. Also discover a very important clue in the chest of map drawers, second drawer from the bottom — half of a torn journal page.

Achenar's Room

Very important: Write down the message from the journal page!

12) If the battery pack runs out of power while you're downstairs, you'll need to fumble through the dark back to the lighthouse, then crank up the generator again.

13) On the way back up the stairs from either brother's room, you'll find a sliding panel on the first landing. (It's marked by a red square.) Click on it to enter the secret compass room.

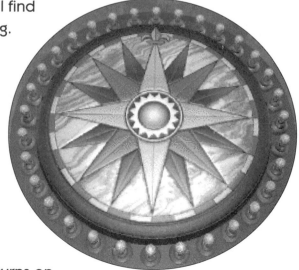

14) When you reach the compass, click on the button corresponding to 135 degrees. (Remember the blinking light in the telescope?) It's the twelfth button clockwise from due north, at the tip of the lower right red ray. This button turns on

the submersible lamp outside the watertight windows, lighting up several underwater chambers.

Note: If you hit the wrong button, the lights go out. Again, you'll have to stumble in the dark back up to the lighthouse, then fire up the generator.

15) Go to the crow's nest and push the left switch to pump out the book room.

16) Return to the ship and go downstairs into the aft hold. (Your way is lighted by the submersible lamp.) Click on the table in the book room. The Myst book will appear.

17) Click on the book to open it, then click again on the picture to return to the Myst Library.

18) OPTIONAL: As always, you can return for the other brother's page. Note: Besides pumping, you also have to crank up the generator and reset the compass to 135 degrees before you can get back down to the book room.

GETTING FROM MYST ISLAND
TO THE MECHANICAL AGE

1) Activate the Marker Switch at the giant sunken gears (if you haven't already), then return to the Library.

2) Now go to the Map. Click and hold on the tower icon until the beam rotates and "locks on" (turns red) over the gear icon.

3) Go to the observatory tower. (If you don't know how yet, refer back to About the Map in the Library.) The lookout slot should be lined up to view the giant gears.

4) Go behind the elevator and climb the ladder with the "key" insignia. The plaque at the top will display the following:

5)

Go to the clocktower site. Use the wheels on the control box by the shore to set the clock on the tower to 2:40.

Note: Each click of the large wheel moves the clock's big hand forward five minutes; each click of the small wheel moves the clock's small hand forward one hour.

6) Push the red button. A gear bridge will rise out of the water.

7) Go across bridge to the clocktower and activate the Marker Switch.

8) Go inside the clocktower. You'll see a gear & lever device with three numbers, set at 3, 3, 3. You need to reset it to 2, 2, 1.

Note: Each lever, left and right, works in two different ways:

PULL AND RELEASE RIGHT LEVER. Moves top two numbers one digit.
PULL AND HOLD RIGHT LEVER. Moves the top number once for every full rotation of middle numbers.
PULL AND RELEASE LEFT LEVER. Moves bottom two numbers one digit.
PULL AND HOLD LEFT LEVER. Moves bottom number once for every full rotation of middle numbers.

Also note: You can only change numbers until the counter-weight on the left wall hits the ground. If that happens, reset the mechanism back to 3, 3, 3 by pulling the handle on the back wall.

9) To enter the correct gear numbers: Pull and release the right lever twice. This gets the "2" on top. Then hold the left lever down. When the "1" appears on the bottom, wait until the middle "2" rotates back around, then release immediately.

10) Go to the giant sunken gears on the other side of the island. The main gear will be open, revealing a secret compartment with the Mechanical transport book.

11) Click on the book to open it and activate the flyby animation, then click on the picture to transport to the Mechanical Age.

MECHANICAL AGE

You begin on the South island. Notice two other islands, North and East. Also notice the control panel next to the giant gear. The main puzzle here is to discover the four-symbol combination which, when loaded into the control panel, gives you access to a hidden room.

1) First, explore both the brothers' rooms. The two pages are hidden in secret storage rooms behind the main rooms.

2) In Sirrus's room, click on the recessed metal panel just to the right of the chair near the floor. The panel opens into a back room.

The Red Page

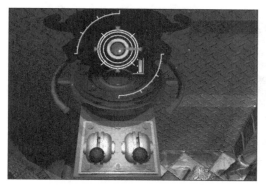

The Fortress Simulator

3) The red page is in the top chest in the back left corner of Sirrus's secret room. Also of interest: A note from Achenar, scrolled and tucked into the wine rack on the right side.

4) In Achenar's room, practice on the fortress rotation simulator before going into the secret room. Then click on the recessed metal panel (marked by a yellow stripe) just to the left of the chair.

5) The blue page is beneath the shelf of poisonous vials and potions on the right side of Achenar's secret room.

6) Go to the back hallway connecting the rooms of Sirrus and Achenar and press the red button.

7) Go down to the elevator control panel. Push the lever; the control hub will rotate. Line up the openings in the two circles on the indicator at the left of the lever. (The circles turn red when properly aligned.)

The Blue Page

The Mechanical Age

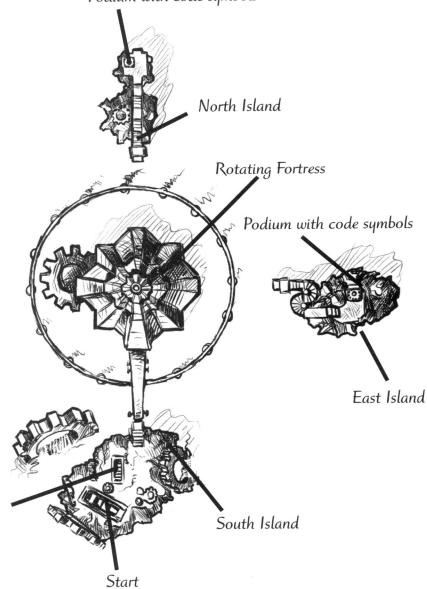

Podium with code symbols

North Island

Rotating Fortress

Podium with code symbols

East Island

Sunken Stairs to
Myst Book

South Island

Start

8) Go back upstairs and press the red button again. When the stairs rise up, get into the elevator and push the up arrow.

9) When you arrive at the top floor, push the middle button, then hurry out. The elevator will drop, revealing the fortress rotation controls.

10) The right handle controls the rotation, the left controls the power. Your goal here is to rotate the fortress entrance ramp to both the North and East islands, where you'll find the two halves of the access code inscribed on podiums. The controls are very sensitive and can be frustrating. All we can say is, keep trying.

Tip: If the rotation gears start spinning wildly out of control, you can stop them by dropping the left "power" handle down to zero and pushing the right "rotation" handle all the way forward. When the gears stop, let the right handle back down gently.

12) The North island has the first half of the code, the East island the second half. Be sure to sketch the symbols.

13) Once you've gotten to both islands, rotate the fortress until it links with the South island (with the giant gear) again. Go to the control panel and enter the four-symbol code — which, if you number the symbols in order, turns out to be 2851.

14) Go down to the secret book chamber. Click on the Myst book to open it, then click on the picture to return to the Myst Library.

GETTING FROM MYST ISLAND
TO THE CHANNELWOOD AGE

    1) Activate the Marker Switch by the log cabin (if you haven't already), then return to the Library.

    2) Now go to the Map. Click and hold on the tower icon until the beam rotates and "locks on" (turns red) over the cabin/tree icon.

    3) Before going to the tower, retrieve the Channelwood book from the bookshelf; it's the green and red one at the far left of the top shelf. Open to the last page and copy the diagram of the tree hut village. Be sure you copy it exactly. Certain important details are not entirely obvious.

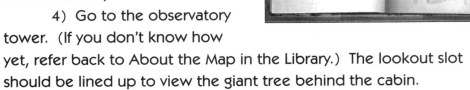

    4) Go to the observatory tower. (If you don't know how yet, refer back to About the Map in the Library.) The lookout slot should be lined up to view the giant tree behind the cabin.

    5) Go behind the elevator and climb the ladder with the "key" insignia. The plaque at the top will display the following combination: "7, 2, 4."

    6) Go in the log cabin and enter 7, 2, 4 into the lock on the safe. Click and drag the handle down to open it.

    7) Click on the matchbox inside the safe. When your cursor turns into a hand holding a match, move it over the flint on the side of the matchbox to "light" the match.

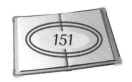
8) Move the "lighted match" cursor over the small box on the bottom left of the furnace. This ignites the pilot light.

9) Click & hold on the right side of the valve wheel until it won't turn anymore and the furnace is fully lit (about 10 or 12 cranks of the wheel). This powers a tree elevator, sending it to the top.

10) Now click & hold on the left side of the valve wheel until the furnace fire is extinguished. IMMEDIATELY hurry out to the giant tree platform — you don't have much time!

11) When the tree elevator's door reaches ground level, click on it to hop in, then ride down to the underground room. There you'll find the Channelwood transport book.

12) Click on the book to open it and activate the flyby animation, then click on the picture to transport to the Channelwood Age.

CHANNELWOOD AGE

The key to this Age is understanding the water power network. You need to redirect water through the piping system on the lower level of

Channelwood in order to power different mechanisms. Simple switching devices are located at almost every Y-fork in the pipes/walkway s. To redirect the flow of water one way or the other, simply click to flip the switch left or right.

Important tip: Make a map of the lower walkways as you go along. It will save you a lot of time. (Of course, this is a strategy guide, and we did include such a map in our Myst Journal.)

1) Work your way to the windmill. Just keep heading toward it — all pipes and pathways lead to it.

2) Inside the windmill, open the spigot at the base of the water tank. (Click on it; it will turn to the left.) You should hear water flowing louder now.

Use switch to redirect water

3) Next, redirect water to the elevator box that leads to the second level. At the first fork from the windmill, direct water left. Then follow this order at succeeding forks: right, right, right.

4) Take the elevator to the second level. (Get in, close door, pull handle.)

Channelwood Lower Level Walkways

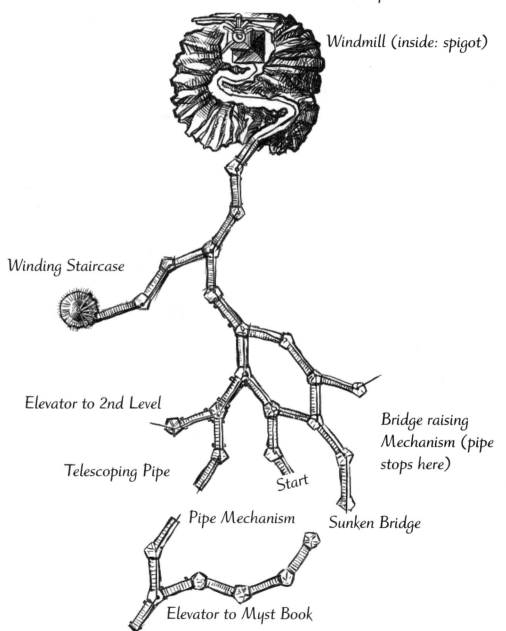

Windmill (inside: spigot)

Winding Staircase

Elevator to 2nd Level

Bridge raising Mechanism (pipe stops here)

Telescoping Pipe

Start

Pipe Mechanism

Sunken Bridge

Elevator to Myst Book

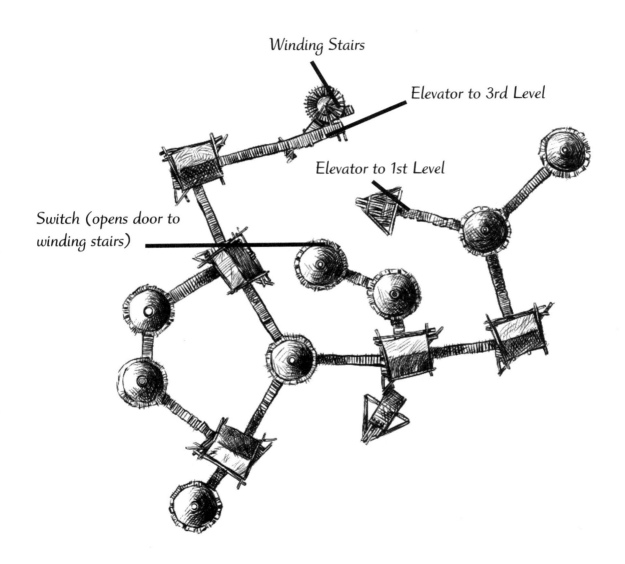

Winding Stairs

Elevator to 3rd Level

Elevator to 1st Level

Switch (opens door to
winding stairs)

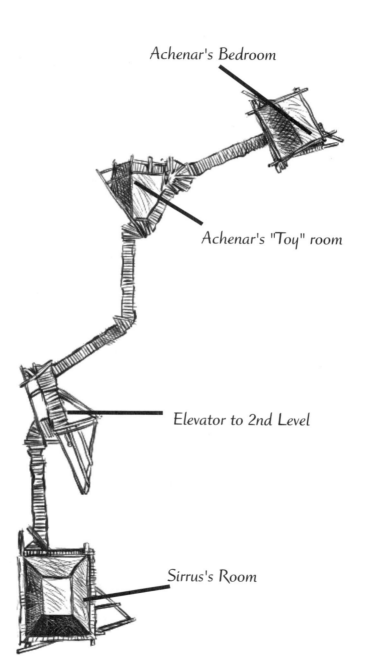

Achenar's Bedroom

Achenar's "Toy" room

Elevator to 2nd Level

Sirrus's Room

5) The sketch you copied from the Channelwood book shows a series of this level of interconnected huts. (So do the maps on the previous pages.) Your task here is to find a way to open the upper and lower gates to the winding staircase so that you can get to the second level without using the elevator.

6) Look on the map. If you copied it correctly, you'll see that one hut is connected to the winding staircase by a dotted line. Go to this hut. (From the elevator, go straight to the first hut, then go right three times, then straight ahead.) In it, you'll find a red switch. Pull the handle on the switch. This opens the gate at the top of the winding staircase.

7) Use the map to work your way to the winding staircase. Go down the stairs and open (just click on) the gate at the bottom. Now follow the walkway back to the first fork.

8) At the first fork, redirect the water right. Then go back up the winding staircase.

The Blue Page

9) Get in the elevator at the top of the winding staircase and take it to the third level.

10) Exit the elevator and follow the walkbridge to Achenar's bedroom — it's the second room down the path. The blue page sits on the floor next to the hologram device.

11) As you return to the elevator you'll see a walkbridge that runs to its right. Follow it to Sirrus's bedroom. The red page is in the drawer of the desk on the left (the one beneath the window that frames the windmill).

12) **Important:** Look also in the right-hand drawer in the pedestal under the bed. There you'll find the other half of the torn

journal page Write it down, combining it with the first half that you found in Achenar's Stoneship bedroom.

13) Take the elevator back down, then go down the winding stairs and out to the first fork.

14) Power up the hidden bridge by directing water at the fork switches and following the flowing water in the following order (beginning with the first fork) — left, left, right.

15) At what seems like a dead end, you'll see that the pipes lead into a mechanism. Pull its handle. The hidden bridge will rise out of the water.

16) Continue down the path to the far elevator, then turn right and follow the other path (the one with water pipes) until you reach the dead end.

17) Turn the crank to telescope the pipe across the gap. Now you can get water power all the way to the far elevator.

18) Go back around to the first Y-fork. Now you can power up the far elevator by directing water in the following order (beginning with the first fork) — left, right, right, left. The water should now be flowing across the telescoped pipe.

19) Go to the far elevator, get in, ride up to the next level. The Myst transport book is just outside the door.

20) Click on the book to open it, then click again on the picture to return to the Myst Library.

21) OPTIONAL: Again, you may want to return to Channelwood for the other brother's page. At the first fork, redirect water right so that you can take the elevator up to the third level, where the bedrooms are. When you get the page, simply return to the first fork and redirect water back left again.

Now you can go straight to the far elevator and return to Myst.

BACK AT MYST: THE ENDGAME

1) Listen to either brother's final message. If you've inserted all four Age pages, he'll tell you about the pattern on p. 158 of the book on the farthest right of the middle shelf.

2) Get the book, turn to page 158, and copy down the pattern.

3) Now it's time to open the Marker Switch Vault. Follow the directions from the torn journal page: Make sure all eight Marker Switches on the island are turned on. Then go to the dock and turn that Marker Switch off. Retrieve the white page from the open vault.

4) Go back to the Library. Enter the fireplace, click the button at the upper left, then enter the pattern on the door. Click the button again to ride up to the secret chamber.

5) When the elevator opens, move forward. Decision time!

6) Defy the brothers by clicking on the green book, then click on the picture of Atrus and listen to his message. When he's finished, click on him again to transport to Dunny. (Be sure you have the white page before you do this!)

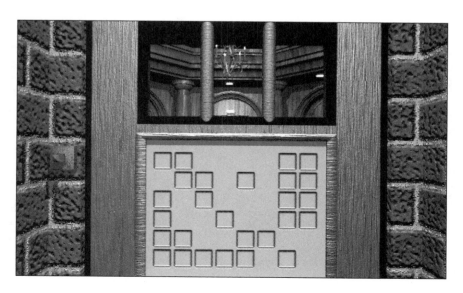

7) In Dunny, give the white page to Atrus when he asks for it.

8) You've won! Now, if you'd like, you can use the Myst book that he offers you to transport back to the Myst Library and explore at your leisure.

The Green Book

The Myst Team

MORE SECRETS OF THE GAMES BOOKS

NOW AVAILABLE

VIDEO GAME BOOKS

Nintendo Games Secrets, Volumes 1, 2, 3, and 4	$12.95 each
Sega Genesis Secrets, Volumes 1, 2, 3, 4, and 5	$12.95 each
Official Sega Genesis Power Tips Book , 2nd Edition (in full color!)	$14.95
Super NES Games Secrets, Volumes 1, 2, 3, and 4	$12.95 each
GamePro Presents:	
Nintendo Games Secrets Greatest Tips	$11.95
Sega Genesis Games Secrets Greatest Tips (Second Edition)	$11.95
Super NES Games Secrets Greatest Tips	$11.95
Super Mario World Game Secrets	$12.95
The Legend of Zelda: A Link to the Past Game Secrets	$12.95
Super Star Wars Official Game Secrets	$12.95
Battletoads: Official Game Secrets	$12.95
Secret of Mana: The Official Strategy Guide	$14.95

Coming Soon:

Sega CD Official Game Secrets	$11.95
3DO Official Consumer's Guide	$14.95

COMPUTER GAME BOOKS

SimEarth: The Official Strategy Guide	$19.95
Harpoon Battlebook: The Official Strategy Guide	$19.95
Wing Commander I and II:	
The Ultimate Strategy Guide	$19.95
Chuck Yeager's Air Combat Handbook	$19.95
The Official Lucasfilm Games	
Air Combat Strategies Book	$19.95
Sid Meier's Civilization,	
or Rome on 640K a Day	$19.95
Ultima: The Avatar Adventures	$19.95
Ultima VII and Underworld: More Avatar Adventures	$19.95
JetFighter II: The Official Strategy Guide	$19.95
A-Train: The Official Strategy Guide	$19.95
PowerMonger: The Official Strategy Guide	$19.95
Global Conquest:The Official Strategy Guide (w/disk)	$24.95
Falcon 3: The Official Combat Strategy Book (w/disk)	$27.95
Dynamix Great War Planes:	
The Ultimate Strategy Guide	$19.95
Gunship 2000: The Authorized Strategy Guide	$19.95
SimLife: The Official Strategy Guide	$19.95
Stunt Island: The Official Strategy Guide	$19.95
Populous: The Official Strategy Guide	$19.95
Prince of Persia: The Official Strategy Guide	$19.95
X-Wing: The Official Strategy Guide	$19.95
Empire Deluxe: The Official Strategy Guide	$19.95
The 7th Guest: The Official Strategy Guide	$19.95
F-15 Strike Eagle III: The Official Strategy Guide	$24.95
Quest for Glory I, II, III, and IV:	
The Authorized Strategy Guide	$19.95
Microsoft Flight Simulator 5 Strategy Guide	$19.95
Strike Commander: The Official Strategy Guide	$19.95

TO ORDER BOOKS ONLY

Please send me the following items:

Quantity	Title	Unit Price	Total
_____	_____	$_____	$_____
_____	_____	$_____	$_____
_____	_____	$_____	$_____
_____	_____	$_____	$_____
_____	_____	$_____	$_____
_____	_____	$_____	$_____
_____	_____	$_____	$_____

	Subtotal	$_____
7.25% SALES TAX California only		$_____
SHIPPING and HANDLING*		$_____
TOTAL ORDER		$_____

*$4.00 shipping and handling charge for the first book, and $0.50 for each additional book.

_____

HOW TO ORDER

By Fax: Call (916) 632-4400.
By Mail: Just fill out the information below and send with your remittance.

My name is_____

I live at_____

City_____ State_____ Zip_____

Visa/MC#_____Exp._____

Signature_____

PRIMA PUBLISHING
P.O. Box 1260BK
Rocklin, CA 95677
(satisfaction unconditionally guaranteed)